Reflections
of Derry

Philip Cunningham

GUILDHALL PRESS

First published in November 2004

Guildhall Press, Unit 15, Ráth Mór Centre,
Bligh's Lane, Derry BT48 0LZ
T: (028) 7136 4413 F: (028) 7137 2949
info@ghpress.com www.ghpress.com

Cover photographs courtesy of John Doherty and David Bigger
Typesetting and cover design by Joe McAllister and Kevin Hippsley
All photographs supplied by author unless otherwise accredited

*This Project is supported by the European Union,
administered by the Local Strategy Partnership
for the Derry City Council Area.*

**EU Programme
for Peace and Reconciliation**
In Northern Ireland and the Border Regions of Ireland

LOCAL STRATEGY PARTNERSHIP
DERRY CITY COUNCIL AREA

Contents

Introduction

Reflections of Derry completes a trilogy of my experiences living in Derry from 1937 until the early 1970s. The first two books, *Derry Down the Days* and *Echoes of Derry*, covering the two decades between my childhood days in 1940 until my marriage in 1960, contained short anecdotes and memories of a more uncomplicated era which conveyed the innocent ways and somewhat happier times for children growing up in the city without the many temptations and dangers that exist today in these so-called modern liberal times. In this book, I have included some extracts and short stories from other Derry peoples' childhood days as well as renewing and enhancing a few of the older, favourite Derry yarns that have been slowly fading out along with the older folks and now my own generation.

I have included a mixture of both older and more recently taken images. You might recognise someone you knew, or even yourself or a relative in one or two of the older pictures; the more recent pictures are a selection of senior Derry people enjoying their retirement years by meeting and chatting to one and other daily in the town centre and shopping foyers. From their relaxed appearances, an appropriate old Derry saying would be, 'They are sticking the times rightly.' Sadly, however, a few of the people seen in some of the more recent images have passed on.

I wish to thank the following who gave me permission to use some of their most cherished memories of youth, precious tales that deserve to be recorded and read and enjoyed by both young and old who maybe will get some inspiration to write down their own bits and pieces of their lives for their own families to enjoy reading: Sister Anna, Lizzie McGarrigle, Gerry Anderson, Claude Wilton, John Keanie, Larry Hasson, Colum Arbuckle and Jim 'Jimbo' McCallion. Thanks also to Stephen Kelly for permission to reproduce extracts from the NSPCC publication *From Acorn to Oak*.

Thanks to Rev Canon Frankie Deeney, Patrick O'Neil, Margaret McGlinchey, Mickey McGuinness, Maura Craig (Central Library, Derry), Eamon Melaugh, David Bigger, John Bryson and Terry Francis for the use of images from their collections, and to those generous people who have loaned me photographs from their own albums and for allowing Guildhall Press to publish them.

Finally, a great deal of gratitude is due to Paul and Kevin Hippsley, Aaron Murray, Michael O'Hanlon, Declan Carlin and Joe McAllister of Guildhall Press and to the many Derry people and friends and acquaintances of mine for giving me the confidence and inspiration to publish *Reflections of Derry* which I hope many will enjoy and add to their own home libraries.

Philip Cunningham

Honeymoon in Dublin

In 1960 I lived in Creggan Estate's Dunree Gardens with my parents, two brothers, three sisters and my mother's brother and sister. Fifteen of us – including a cousin, two step-brothers and a step-sister, all part of my father's first family – had moved to the estate in 1950 from Friel's Terrace, a row of nine houses at the top of the banking overlooking the old Bogside where at one time our household numbered eighteen.

The chronic unemployment among men in the city was beginning to improve slightly in 1960 with the BSR at full production and the opening of the Du Pont factory at Maydown. I was already employed as a lorry helper in WG O'Doherty's stout bottling and distributors store in Bishop Street, which was owned by Jimmy Toland who resided with his family in 2 Abercorn Road. Hugh McAnee, the lorry driver, along with his wife Agnes, owned the Silver Dog Bar at the bottom of Bishop Street.

In September 1960, I married Rosita Heaney from Pennyburn in St Patrick's Church at nine o'clock in the morning. Father Gildea, who was the curate in charge, performed the wedding ceremony and our reception was held at eleven o'clock in Stevenson's Restaurant in the Strand Road. A local baritone called William Loughlin just happened to be delivering laundry to the premises and he sang a few of the popular favourite songs of the time for the guests. The reception ended at a quarter to twelve and we went to the Great Northern Railway (GNR) station in Foyle Road to catch the 12.45pm train to honeymoon in Dublin where we stayed in a bed and breakfast house in Glasnevin for five days. I remember the house was just a hundred yards down the road from the front gates of the famous cemetery, and that's where we spent our first day, visiting the graves of some of those who died during the 1916 Irish rebellion.

On our first night, we were wakened at four o'clock by the sounds of hundreds of clattering hooves and cows bellowing. On looking out of the window, we saw a gigantic herd of cattle being driven along by a few collie dogs and some men with sticks. We didn't sleep too soundly the rest of the night and I learned the next morning that thousands of animals were herded through the streets of Dublin every week to the North Wall at the docks to be loaded onto ships for exportation to England.

Nelson's Column was a big attraction for visitors to the city in those days, and Rosita and I went up the spiral staircase inside to enjoy the lofty view of O'Connell Street and surrounding city. The IRA blew up the pillar in 1966. The Guinness Brewery was the other place we visited, and at that time the old wooden barrels were being gradually replaced by aluminium casks. At the end of that tour, I came out starry-eyed after sampling a few bottles of their free stout in the brewery's bar.

One evening in our bedroom, my curiosity prompted me to have a closer examination of the furniture that must have been over fifty years old, when I noticed an old square biscuit tin on top of the wardrobe. I carefully lifted it down and blew away the thick layer of dust from the lid which made my wife and me take fits of sneezing. As I opened it, I felt guilty at delving into what might have been someone else's secret hiding place. Inside, there were a handful of revolver bullets and some old photographs that were in perfect condition. Some of the people's faces were ringed with pencil marks. On the back of the photographs were names, which, I presumed, were of those men in the pictures. I recognised Éamon de Valera, Arthur Griffiths and Patrick Pearse, who had been rebel leaders at the beginning of the 1916 uprising in Dublin. Patrick Pearse and his brother William were executed by firing squad along with thirteen other Irishmen in Kilmainham Jail for their part in the uprising. In all, ninety death sentences were passed, but not all were carried out. I closed the tin and replaced it on top of the wardrobe, curtailing my curiosity in case I uncovered any more private artefacts.

Early Housing Conditions

Housing in Derry in the 1950s and '60s was chronically scarce with only a few new houses being built for families from the old overcrowded streets of crumbling habitations. Many newly married couples were either going to England, living in a room in their parents' homes or with some relations, or renting a room in one of the old condemned tenement houses or above some shop. Springtown Camp, which lay outside the city boundary on the Buncrana Road, was full of

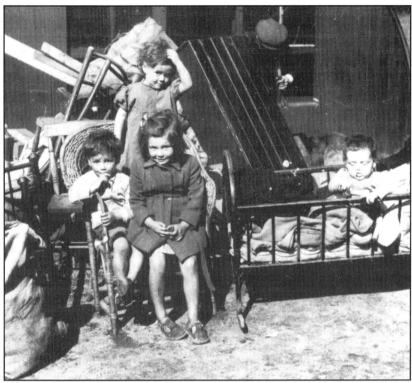

One of the many homeless Derry families who squatted into Springtown Camp in 1946 after it was vacated by the American Forces at the end of the war. (Courtesy Michael McGuinness)

deprived and abandoned Derry families; other families were even being allocated caravans in the Brandywell Showgrounds in Ann Street.

John McGinley from Blucher Street married Maureen Doherty from Ann Street – a little street that ran off Abbey Street – around the same time that we were married, and were also homeless like hundreds of other young couples. After spending a few days in John's family home, they were offered a back bedroom in his aunt Kitty McKane's house in Lecky Road. Kitty was also a cousin of mine and I knew that she had four daughters and a son living in the small two-storey house at the junction of St Columb's Street and the Lecky Road; the gable end of the house is still standing there today and is now widely known as the Free Derry Wall.

Free Derry Wall, Lecky Road, in 1969. Note the graffiti on the wall of the bookmaker's shop at the bottom of Wellington Street: 'We want better odds, signed Ned Kelly.' (Courtesy Rev Frank Deeney)

Living With Cassie Gallagher

Accepting what seemed to us as normal, we went to stay with my wife's old spinster grand-aunt Cassie Gallagher, a former seamstress who lived at 302 Bishop Street, near the bottom end. She was the sister of my wife's deceased grandfather, Mickey 'The Hawk' Gallagher, who worked as a guardsman on the GNR along with the Sweeney brothers, Johnny, Danny and George, who also lived in the locality.

The house wasn't overly furnished, the toilet being in the backyard. Our upstairs front bedroom had a square piece of linoleum in the middle of the floor and a small chest of drawers between the two windows, the bed being the only other piece of furniture. I painted the bare floorboards around the outside of the lino with brown paint and made a small bedside table from a wooden orange box by standing it on its end and hanging a small curtain over the front of it. I also nailed a piece of white linoleum on top and made a bedside lamp from an empty green chartreuse liqueur bottle that I got from WG O'Doherty's bottling store. Beside the lamp, I set my alarm clock, which would waken us in the mornings to go to work; my wife Rosita in Welch Margetson's shirt factory in Carlisle Road and me in the bottling stores that faced Adair's Funeral Parlour in Bishop Street.

Electric lighting was only installed in the living-room and in our bedroom. In the darkness of night, I used to get an eerie feeling whenever I rose to go downstairs to the toilet in the backyard. Whenever old Cassie was going to bed, she was dressed in a long grey nightdress with her brushed, silvery-white hair, which she usually had tied up in a bun, hanging loosely about her shoulders and down her back. I got the shivers whenever I saw her coming up the stairs to her bedroom, because she carried a lighted candle in one of those old candleholders that were to be seen in illustrations from Charles Dickens's stories. Her long flickering shadow crept along the wall as she silently flitted up the stairs and into her small bedroom that overlooked the river and the railway tracks behind the high wall that ran parallel to Foyle Road at the back of the house.

Above: O'Brien's Bar, Lecky Rd, at the bottom of McKeown's Lane, 1956. (Courtesy Margaret McGlinchey)

Left: Mrs Duffy talking to Johnny McGovern as he holds a roll of linoleum in the Lecky Road beside Rossville Street in 1956.

11

After she closed her bedroom door, I could hear her knees softly coming into contact with the wooden floor and I knew that she was kneeling there at her bedside, saying her night prayers before she settled down to sleep. The fragrance of the burning candle wax drifted through the entire upper storey and into our room, and I drifted off to sleep with memories of my younger days when my mother led us up to bed with the light of the candle chasing the ghosts away from the dark corners of the staircase and our bedroom.

We were quite contented living in our temporary home with Cassie until about a month went by and she began to act very strangely towards me. The first rare occurrence we noticed was when we went to the cinema one evening and returned to find that our key wouldn't open the front door. We were locked out and began to knock, hoping Cassie would come and unbolt the door. As I was knocking at the door, we heard her calling weakly to us from the inside, 'Go away. I don't want that man back into this house again.' My wife pleaded with her for nearly half an hour to let us in but couldn't convince her that the strange man was Phil, who had been living there for the past four weeks. Two of the neighbours from across the street, Dinny Holmes and Harry Barton, as well as Minnie Smith who lived beside Mickey Lynch's pub, came out on hearing us calling to Cassie and, on learning of our plight, finally persuaded her to open the door to us. She was wearing her long, grey nightdress and never spoke to me as I entered. She scurried down the hallway and up the stairs with her lighted candle casting long, wavering shadows on the ceiling and walls, leaving a thin, trailing vapour of smoke in her wake.

A few days afterwards, I came in from work and was sitting with my wife at the table, eating my dinner. Cassie was sitting beside the fire range with the poker in her hand and began to rattle it against the bars of the grate. I looked over at her and she was staring wide-eyed at me, and her lips were tightly pursed. I was feeling slightly uneasy and kept glancing at her out of the corner of my eye as I hastily finished my meal. Suddenly, she screamed and waved the poker at me as I bolted from my chair and made for the door. My wife went to her and, taking the poker from her hand, asked what was wrong with her carrying on like that, as she was never aggressive before and had always been a gentle old lady. Cassie whispered loudly in answer, 'That strange man you brought in here is wearing my teeth and eating with them.' We burst out laughing and I showed her that my teeth were my own and invited her to try and tug them out. After we convinced her that she had been mistaken, she became her timid ladylike self again.

Little unforeseen and unexplainable minor incidents happened more frequently after that, and a couple of weeks later came the last straw for me. My wife and I were wakened one Saturday at the early hour of six o'clock in the morning by what sounded to me like the wailing of a Banshee coming from downstairs. The hairs were standing on the back of my neck as I pulled on my trousers to follow my wife down the gloomy stairs to investigate. I deliberately let my wife lead the way in case I might have met a female and may have embarrassed us both if the woman wasn't in a proper state of respectable attire. Cassie's bedroom door was closed, as it always was, and we didn't expect her to be awake so early. At the bottom of the stairs, the wailing became weaker as my wife opened the living-room door and we both warily stepped inside, not knowing what to expect. My heart was pounding in my throat and I became even more frightened when I saw old Cassie standing on the table with her back to us, crying out of the window. My wife went to her first and discovered what was causing Cassie's unnatural behaviour: Cassie had her hands caught between the upper and lower sections of the sash window.

Bishop Street youths posing on what was locally called the Donkey Island banking in 1945. Includes: Pat McCarron, Patsy McIntyre, Paddy Farren, Kathleen McNaught, Sally Farren, James McCarron, Harry Francis, John McCarron, Joe Devine, Joe McCarron, Paddy Starrs and Terry Francis. (Courtesy Terry Francis)

After I managed to release her trapped hands, which had purple bruises across her thin, bony fingers, she told us that she had risen at five o'clock and come downstairs to make a cup of tea. She had forgotten to turn off the gas tap under the teapot, with the result that the pot went dry and the tea leaves burned, causing the room to fill with smoke. Then she climbed onto the table to let the top sash of the window down to air the room, and as she did so, the window cord broke, causing the top sash to fall and trap her fingers and she was too frail to release her hands. Cassie had been in pain since five-thirty until we were wakened by her cries for help. I could have cried myself as I listened to her, and it was then we realised that old Cassie needed more than her bruised hands attended to.

We stayed with Cassie for another month, and during that time, we learned that the poor old dear was beginning to suffer from a disease I'd never heard of before: senile dementia. The last time we spoke to Cassie Gallagher, she was being tenderly cared for in the hospital before we went to live with my wife's grandparents, Pat and Mary Heaney, in Oak Villa at the corner of New Street and the Racecourse Road in Pennyburn.

Life in Oak Villa

Oak Villa was the name of Pat and Mary Heaney's home that he and his son Jim built when Pat retired, aged seventy, as a ships' joiner in Lisahally. He made all the kitchen and bedroom furniture himself and had a small vegetable garden at the rear of the house where he built two greenhouses in which he grew tomatoes. The little two-storey house had two bedrooms. The smallest, where Rosita and I slept, measured ten feet by eight. There was a small kitchen and an equally small living-room, where there was a cream enamelled range on which most of the cooking was done. A sitting-room, only rarely used, was crammed with outdated furniture. In the evenings, after pottering about in his garden and greenhouses, Pat sat in his easy chair in front of the range where Mary tended to him hand and foot, serving him meals and leaving his pipe and tobacco handy for him as well as

Pupils of St Patrick's school in the 1950s. Back L to R: N Boyle, B McDermott, W McWilliams, P O'Connell, Unknown, M Cassidy, J Nicell, R Quigley, Po Hagan, H McCourt and D Kineton. Middle L to R: W Mullen, J Laverty, J McCarron, H Harkin, B McGeady, P McGrory, B Rabbett, R Matchett, P McKeever and C McGeady. Front L to R: D McGinley, G Lynch, E Porter, M McCaul, H Brown, Teacher Fred Campbell, T Doherty, A Norrby, J Burke, D McQuilkin and K Kerr.

(Courtesy Terry Francis)

keeping the fire going. She often scolded him for leaving brown tobacco stains on the front of the range where he spat every so often through the bars of the grate into the fire.

Every Saturday morning, Mary carried out the same ritual cleaning of the house and wouldn't accept anybody else's assistance. She cleaned the range thoroughly both inside and out after spreading sheets of newspaper over the whole floor, and put the soot into a large paper sack and placed it in the dustbin. The pine kitchen table got scoured with Vim and warm water and the insides of all the windows cleaned before the floors were scrubbed. While all that was happening, Pat made himself scarce to the greenhouses, and I went out on my bicycle until the Angelus bells were announcing noon. Then we knew it was safe to enter the house again when everything was clean and sparkling and the appetising aroma of a simmering pot of soup wafted through the house as well as drifting out through the open back door and kitchen window. Meanwhile, Rosita was in the town, shopping for the weekend's meat and groceries.

Without a television in the living-room, we passed many enjoyable evenings playing draughts and listening to a radio programme or to Pat's collection of long-playing records. His favourite one was Brendan O'Dowda's Irish selection, *On The One Road*. All the while, Mary was busy sitting at her Singer sewing machine making patchwork quilts or clothes for herself and her grandchildren, and the wee house was stifling hot with the heat coming from the stoked-up fire in the range. Our baby, Patrick, the first of our family of six sons and one daughter, was born six months after going to live in Oak Villa in June 1961, and his coming caused great pride and joy to us, and especially to Pat and Mary, who were his great-grandparents.

Now and then as he sat in front of the range smoking his pipe, Pat told us about amusing events and related incidents that happened in Derry in his younger days. One such tale he told us often was about a hunchbacked cobbler who worked in Creggan Street when Pat had a small joinery workshop in a shed behind one of the houses there in the early 1920s from where he made and sold furniture. The following tale is as much as I can remember about the story.

Harry's Wake

Harry Milligan, a retired shoemaker, was a seventy-nine-year-old bachelor who lived alone in the small one-storey house in a little narrow street that ran off William Street where he was born. He had lived there with his widowed mother, Lila, who survived to the ripe old age of eighty-six. His father, Dessie, joined the British army when Harry was only one year old and never returned to Derry, being declared missing somewhere in Europe.

When Harry was one and a half years old, he had his spine injured in a fall when his uncle Henry was playfully throwing him up to the ceiling and catching him, a little game that all children experienced and enjoyed as babies. Uncle Henry had been at a wedding earlier that day and was slightly under the weather from drinking a little more whiskey than he was capable of holding. He called in to see Lila and Harry on his way home and lifted the baby from its cot to have a bit of fun with him. He threw him gently up towards the ceiling a few times until he stumbled as he caught Harry and fell with him grasped tight in his arms. The two crashed to the floor with the baby underneath, crushing him against the edge of the fire fender. Medical aid was not widely available or very advanced in those days, and Lila didn't realise that her son's spine was damaged. As Harry grew older, he developed a hunched back as a result of the fall.

During his youth, Harry was cruelly teased by many unthinking boys (and sometimes girls) about his deformity, and many times when he came home, he would burst into tears as he told his mother about some of the cruel remarks called at him in the playground and in the streets. When he became a teenager, Harry grew more confident in himself and learned, through his painful experiences, how to avoid the hateful people and also to create friendships with many of the more understanding ones by always having a cheerful and friendly smile, although hard to do on many occasions.

All through his teenage years and adult life, he learned that there were good and bad people everywhere, and that most, no matter how healthy or perfectly shaped they were, at one time or another were bullied and hurt by cruel individuals. Harry just got on with his life as normally as possible, working as a cobbler in Houston's shoemaker's shop near the bottom of Creggan Street, and in his leisure hours after work in the evenings would be seen helping the sacristan with his duties in and around St Columba's Church, locally referred to as the Long Tower Chapel. On his way home each evening from the church after doing his good-deed services, Harry always dropped into William Mailey's bar in Holywell Street for a bottle of stout and a half-glass of fortified South African wine and a chat with the locals. Friday nights were an exception in the bar when most of the customers, including Harry, changed their usual order of a bottle of stout and a half of wine to a bottle of wine and a half-glass of stout. The craic would reach ninety with Harry acting like Quasimodo in *The Hunchback of Notre Dame* and the rest of the bar clients egging him on until he would attempt to swing from the ceiling light and then get put out of the bar by the frustrated barman, who then had to settle down the others who never were punished for their parts in starting the whole shenanigans every Friday night.

One day, another shoe repair shop opened up in Creggan Street, just opposite the main gates of St Eugene's Cathedral. This event caused a bit of alarm in Houston's, because the owner of the new shop, Alfie Hay, was a Protestant who happened to be of a different religious persuasion from most of the other residents in the area, and through his good manners, hard work and first-class repairing, he gradually gained enough custom to make a livelihood for himself and his family, who lived in the Lower Road. But in the end, Hay's new shop never affected Houston's trade, because there was ample work for cobblers in those days when everybody wore leather shoes or boots and had them mended numerous times until they eventually were past wearing and then passed down to some more needy persons who couldn't even afford to buy themselves a pair of the cheapest imported shoes.

At nine o'clock one morning, as Harry was hunched over his shoemaker's last, mending a boot, Jim Healey, a customer, came into the shop and casually said, 'It's not hard to know that the biggest day of the year for Protestants – the Twelfth of August – is next week when they march round Derry's Walls beating their Lambeg drums, for I see Alfie Hay has put a sign in his shop window insulting our bishop.' Harry paused his hammering and asked Jim what he was talking about and Jim said, 'A big sign with words in thick black print that says: *Cobblers to Bishop McHugh*. What do you think of that?'

'I don't believe it,' answered Harry as he stopped working.

Harry stood up and went to the door to look up the street where he saw three people standing looking wide-eyed into Hay's window; he went up the street to have a look for himself. His jaw dropped when he read the notice inside, pressed up against the glass for every passer-by to see: *Cobblers to Bishop McHugh*. He was very annoyed and rushed down to his own place, whereupon he immediately got a large piece of white card and proceeded to write with a thick black crayon. When he completed the notice, he stood the card in the window and, cursing under his breath, went back to his last to finish the boots for Mr Houston to come in and pick up and deliver to one of his best customers, Justin McCarthy, the Nationalist MP for Westminster.

For the next half-hour, customers came and went without mentioning the notices in any of the windows and Harry knew that everyone in the neighbourhood would regard him as the defender of their beloved Lordship, Bishop McHugh, who didn't deserve to be insulted by a bigoted, blow-in Protestant and flute player in the Lower Road pipe band who would be marching round the Walls the following week playing kick-the-pope tunes.

Mr Houston, on his way to his shop that morning, saw the sign in Hay's window as he was passing and went in to bid the time of day, as well as to hear what Alfie's reason was for the advertisement about mending the bishop's footwear. Alfie told him that the bishop had come in a couple of days before and said he wanted to show his genuine ecumenical feelings and would like to give a good example to his own congregation and to Mr Hay's people. Therefore, as a true Christian gesture, and for the advancement of cross-community neighbourliness, he requested Alfie to mend four pairs of fine leather shoes for him, which he did, and that is when he got the idea to put the sign in the window. Mr Houston, although being slightly jealous, wished Alfie well and left the shop knowing that Bishop McHugh would resume having his shoes repaired by Harry as he had being doing since he came into the diocese.

Mr Houston was later than usual, coming into the shop at eleven to pick up McCarthy's boots. He bid Harry good morning as he always did and asked, 'Did you read the notice in Mister Hay's window?'

'I did,' Harry answered. 'And did you read the better notice that I put into our shop window, Mr Houston?' Harry replied with a broad smile on his face, proudly pushing out his chest to straighten his hump.

Mr Houston frowned questionably as he scratched his chin without saying a word, then quickly made for the street to look into his shop window to read the sign. After reading it, his face seemed to freeze over, turning white, and his eyes opened wide in disbelief. Then he began to bless himself and thump his chest as he loudly said, 'Jesus, Mary and Joseph, are you trying to ruin us, Harry?' The message written on the white card seemed to scream through the shop window at him: *Bollocks to the Archbishop of Canterbury.*

The sign was swiftly removed from the window and Mr Houston was relieved that not too many people had seen it. Because the notice had only been there for a brief time that morning, no damage had been done and he warned Harry never to place one there again without firstly letting him see it or he would be sacked. Harry didn't attempt to make any excuse for his stupidity in listening to narrow-minded people as he nodded in agreement to his boss's chastisements. He bent even lower over his last and looked more hunchbacked than usual as he placed a piece of leather on an upturned shoe. An unseen tear rolled down Harry's cheek and fell onto the new piece of leather. The tear-stained damp spot darkened and spread as it was absorbed to eventually fade away like all of the many other tears that Harry had shed onto life's tapestry.

Harry worked diligently at his trade until he was finally forced to retire at sixty after he contracted a serious illness in his lungs by breathing in too much leather dust over the years working at the lathe and sewing machine – an ailment that was common among cobblers in those years.

Then, at seventy-nine, Harry's lungs could not function normally anymore, and after spending a brief time in St Columb's Chest Hospital, which used to be in St Columb's Park in the Waterside, he breathed his last. Having no next of kin, his former employer, Mr Houston, had McClafferty's undertakers arrange the wake and funeral. Harry was duly dressed and laid out in his Sunday suit on the bed in the front bedroom of his little home in the Bogside where he had slept since he was a young boy. One slight adjustment had to be made by the undertaker while dressing the corpse, which still had the handicap of a hump that made it difficult to lay it out flat as normal. A long strap had to be discreetly placed across the chest and secured under the bed to hold the top half of the body down.

That evening, the wake house was packed with Harry's old friends from Mailey's public house and many of his other acquaintances and neighbours, who had made sandwiches and tea. They soon took to serving out the whiskey and bottles of stout and cigarettes that Harry had stocked up for his own use when he would be too weak to go for a drink and chat with the men in his local bar. As the evening wore on, the craic was getting merrier and noisier among the Mailey's men and a few neighbours. Any stranger who might have been passing would have thought that a wedding party was in full swing, there were so many sounds of gaiety and loud laughter coming out through the open front door and window.

At five minutes to midnight, the Mailey's men were swapping stories with some of the neighbours about the pranks they used to play on Harry and teasing him about his hunched appearance. The whole front room was erupting in a riot of noise and laughter as Fat Packie Boyle ambled up and down the floor hunched over like an ape as he mimicked Harry while relating to the watery-eyed chuckling spectators one of the many times he had tormented 'Harry the Hunch'. Halfway through his story, he suddenly froze when he looked towards the room door to see Father Mullan, who had come to say prayers for the happy repose of the soul of Harry Milligan, staring at him with anger on his face. The room went silent as the priest looked into everybody's guilt-ridden eyes, one at a time, until he reached the last person, who began to shuffle his feet and hide his face in his hands.

'We were just having a wee laugh,' Fat Packie meekly whimpered, breaking the silence.

'Having a wee laugh, is that what you all call it?' Father Mullan bellowed. 'It's not enough that you all taunted the poor deformed being all his life and made him feel miserable,' spittles of anger splattering those sitting nearest to him, 'but you all have the audacity and bloody downright cheek to drink his whiskey and smoke his cigarettes while you still mock and laugh about the innocent wee soul lying there on his deathbed that never harmed or said an ill word about any one of you blackguards in all of his living days. Him who helped us out in the church and did nothing but charitable works for the poor and the more unfortunate of God's children in this holy town of St Columba's Derry.'

He slammed the door shut and paced across the room, brushing cowering Fat Packie out of his way with his shoulder, and stopped beside the bed where Harry lay with a slight angelic smile on his lips and a pair of black rosary beads entwined through the fingers of his joined hands on top of his breast. Most of the shamed men crept slowly nearer to the now closed door in readiness for a quick exit as soon as the midnight prayers for Harry would finish. Father Mullan bent over the corpse and made a sign of the cross on its forehead before blessing himself as he began the introductory prayer for the rosary: 'Thou, O Lord, wilt open my lips.'

The men responded in low tones, 'And my tongue shall announce Thy praise.'

In the silent moment before the priest began the first decade of the rosary, the sound of a loud, sharp crack came from under the bed and Harry sat up with his hands joined together under his chin, the innocent smile still on his countenance. Not realising that the strap holding Harry down flat on the bed had snapped with the heat and the strain, everyone panicked with fright at seeing his corpse coming back to life before their very eyes and the Mailey's men stampeded screaming for the door. Fat Packie was the first to grab the handle and pull the door open, only to be swept out into the street by the wave of frightened, heaving bodies behind him.

As the crowd ran scared from the wake room, Father Mullan was frozen to the spot with fright, the hair standing on the back of his neck with the shock of seeing the dead Harry coming back to life. But the priest quickly recovered and dashed for the now half-open door to escape the horrible miracle. As he squeezed through the narrow opening, the inside handle of the door caught his trailing coat pocket, pulling the door tightly closed behind him. With his coat pocket snagged on the handle inside, and he trying to pull it free from the outside, a wave of uncontrollable fear swept through the priest as he envisaged Harry clutching the coat in the quiet, creepy room where a few minutes before there was merrymaking and laughter.

'Let me go, Harry,' he screeched. 'In the name of God, please release me,' he began to splutter. But only silence on the other side. And Father Mullan didn't have the courage to open the door to face the dead man come to life, even with all the protection he thought he had from all the angels in Heaven.

He began to tremble, and in desperation he screamed through the door, 'Let go of my coat, Harry, you humpy wee bastard!'

All of a sudden, he heard a tearing sound and he fell back against the wall as the end of his coat was released to slide through the narrow gap at the side of the still closed door. The shaken priest joined the rest of the relieved parishioners who had been silently watching and listening to Father Mullan's whole predicament in the hallway of Harry Milligan's wake house.

The women, who had been serving the refreshments, were in the back living-room tidying up and chatting among themselves when they heard the commotion from the wake room and Father Mullan's shouts and swears at Harry; three of them dashed out to investigate. By the time they got out into the hallway, everything was over and Mrs Coyle opened the door. Followed by the other two, she went in to see if there were any men sitting with the corpse and found the room empty and silent except for Harry, who was still reposing peacefully on his bed.

The priest and the group of men watched the three women entering the room and coming out again. Mrs Coyle was in front, and she came to the front door holding up a ragged piece of black cloth. 'I think this is a part of your coat pocket, Father,' she calmly said as she looked at Father Mullan, who coughed gently and tried to hide his red face by lowering his gaze towards his feet. 'It was hanging on the handle of the room door, your reverence,' she continued as she went towards him to place it into his outstretched hand.

'Thank you, Mrs Coyle. I just had a wee accident and I'm sure that everybody would like to go into the wake room again and say the rest of the prayers for Harry.' Which they all did, and not one word was mentioned about the unmanly scenes that had occurred that evening.

Four American servicemen purchasing milk from roundsman Joe Lynch outside the gate lodge of Boomhall House in the Culmore Road in 1944. The McCarron family, whose son Pat was a top jockey in England, lived in the gatehouse, and the milk cart belonged to Robert McCarter from Culmore. (Courtesy Susan Lynch)

On the morning of the funeral, Father Mullan stood among the Mailey's men at the graveside as Father Browne led the prayers over Harry's coffin. The burial over, people slowly drifted away, leaving a small group of men silently praying and bidding their own private last farewells over Harry Milligan's wreath-laden grave. It was the Mailey's men, with Father Mullan in their midst, and when their private prayers were said, they all walked along together reminiscing about the laughs they used to have with Harry when he was hale and hearty.

Father Mullan had his tale to refresh as well about that night at the wake when he chastised everyone in the room for the jokes they played on Harry the Hunch and then discovered that he himself was just as human and vulnerable as any other man when he caught his coat pocket on the door handle.

On leaving the cemetery, they all visited Mailey's to drink a last farewell to their old buddy, and I'm sure that as Father Mullan put his half-pint of stout to his lips to drink a toast to his memory, Harry Milligan was swinging with the aid of his angel's wings from the barroom ceiling light as he smiled down upon them all.

It was quite an incredible tale, and I've heard incomplete similar pieces of it told over the years by other younger people who heard it from their grandparents.

Hurricane Debbie

One Saturday afternoon in 1961, everyone in the Oak Villa household attended to their own activities: Mary rolling out a slab of fresh dough to bake scone bread; Pat sharpening his saw in his work shed; Rosita just arriving in from the town, and me standing reading the *Irish News* at the kitchen window that looked out towards New Street, a row of single-storey houses that used to be called 'Jam Pot Row' by the people of old Shantallow.

I noticed a north-westerly breeze beginning to blow in strong gusts that caused pieces of straw and paper to chase round in circles and then sent them all flying above the rooftops in the street. The boughs and tops of the tall beech trees that stood in the planting behind New Street and at the side of Oak Villa began to toss about, sending showers of fresh leaves swirling and skittering across the open field behind them. It was then I saw a little man called Charlie McCarron from Springtown Camp who came round the streets every Saturday pushing his handcart. It was loaded with chopped sticks for fire kindling that he sold for a penny a bundle to the housewives in the Collon and Pennyburn districts.

The breeze got stronger until it became a gale, and I went out to the garden and called to Pat that he should come into the house in case the glass of the greenhouse blew in on top of him. I then called to Charlie that he would be safer to put his handcart in the lane behind New Street and to make his way indoors, because I could hear the cracks of breaking twigs and small branches as the wind wrenched them from the swaying trees. As I called to him, his handcart was tossed into the air with a strong gust and the sticks scattered along the ground. He tried to rescue his merchandise but got bowled over himself, and when he got to his feet again, he ran across the street like a hare, with the wind pushing him from behind. I don't know where he ended his journey and it was too dangerous to go after him, because by now a storm was raging, and huge branches and treetops were snapping off. Frequently, above the howling wind, I could hear loud crackling noises coming from the line of trees that bordered the planting along the Racecourse and Culmore Roads as another tree was uprooted or had its trunk snapped like a matchstick.

The storm lasted for almost four hours and reports that evening were about the vast amount of damage wreaked, destroying property and forests throughout Ireland and all over the British Isles. In Derry, many roofs and buildings needed major repairs and twenty-one trees came down along the Derry to Moville road. It was all the more dangerous because no-one was prepared for it, the weathermen previously forecasting fine weather and slight breezes not knowing that Hurricane Debbie, one of the most devastating for many years, was to pay us an unexpected and unwelcome visit.

Sharing a Bed

Jimmy Lynch, my pal since boyhood who lived in Fox's Corner, married Mary Melarky from Ballyoan, near Campsie in the Waterside. Like us, they were trying to find a permanent home in which to rear a family, when one came along. They rented a bed-sitting-room in a large house owned by Cullens, who had an amusement arcade in Buncrana.

Jimmy and Mary invited us to their place one Saturday evening, and my wife and I went on a bus from the Guildhall Square to visit their bed-sit and found that they were happy to have found a place to live. The room was quite spacious and well furnished, with a large comfortable settee and two chairs and a king-size bed in one corner, and the cooking and dining area with a dining table and four chairs in the other. We were all teetotallers then, as money was scarce and the drinking culture not in vogue in those days.

The evening was spent chatting and having our teas, listening to their collection of popular records that Jimmy played on his BSR turntable and to the radio until it was time to go home. At ten o'clock, we remembered that the last bus to the town had left at nine-thirty and as it was too far for us to walk home, they persuaded us to stay the night with them. At bedtime, we borrowed some night clothes and all retired to the same king-size bed, Mary and Rosita lying beside each other in the middle and Jimmy and me on the outsides. We were all very innocent and modest, as were most of the young people in those days, and everyone fell asleep in the big, comfortable, warm bed until nine o'clock the next morning. After our breakfasts of porridge, tea and toast, we caught the bus to the Waterside and went to eleven o'clock Mass and Holy Communion in St Columb's Church.

Pennyburn Shops and Springtown Camp

Pennyburn in the early 1960s wasn't the built-up and congested place it is today and road traffic was very light. No new housing estates were built until 1963/64, the first being Belmont for families of RUC members and a selection of other people. The only small clusters of old homes past the

Fox's Corner residents in June 1950 outside Ned McDevitt's house and the entrance to McAdam's Close. McCrossan's pawnshop can be seen in the background. The back row includes: Maggie 'Harkin' Rooney, Sarah Daisy, Vincent Harkin, Nana McGowan, Kathleen McDaid, Markie McLaughlin, Seamus McDevitt, Anthon Rodgers, M Doherty, Ned McDevitt and Bella McLaughlin. The middle and front rows include: Paddy Havelin, Jean 'Lynch' McCallion, Jane Smith, May Doherty and Kathleen and Isobel McLaughlin. (Courtesy Billy and Jean McCallion)

28

The Corinthians FC, Collon, in the early 1950s. Back L to R: T Taylor, S Hamilton, A Goodman, B Downey, K Cassidy, B Doherty and C Ming. Front L to R: W Goodman, W Taylor, L Gray, C Baird, T Stewart, R Boardman, C Stewart and W Downey. The picture was taken at Buncrana Road. (Courtesy Terry Francis)

old Shantallow pub (owned at the time by Aidan Barrett) were Tin Town, Shamrock Row and Steelstown and Ballyarnett Villages. The majority of those residents walked or cycled to church and to the new St Patrick's school at the junction of the Collon Lane and Racecourse Road.

At the bottom of the Racecourse Road were Barney Norrby's grocery and confectionery shop, Willie McGowan's fish and chip shop, Bertie Downey the shoemaker, Brian McCloskey the chemist, and beside Eddie Diggin's bar at the Collon was Albert Goodman's newsagent and confectionery shop. A few hundred yards from the Collon on the Buncrana Road were Joe Heaney's Maybrook Dairy and the Springtown Camp, consisting of 180 Nissen huts abandoned by USA forces at the end of the war in 1945. The huts were immediately occupied by hundreds of homeless and impoverished Derry families who were then classed as squatters to be left to their fate by Derry Corporation and County Councils. The families endured atrocious living conditions and neglect by the authorities and were shunned by many Derry people for over twenty years.

To give a Springtown address to a potential employer meant that the Springtown person's chances of getting work were greatly diminished or

Left: Bertie Downey in 1998 on the occasion of his 70th year as a shoemaker working in his shop in Pennyburn. (Courtesy Lorcan Doherty)

Right: A campaign leaflet distributed by the residents of Springtown Camp to highlight their awful living conditions in 1964.

AN APPEAL
TO
THE PEOPLE OF DERRY

1—The residents of Springtown Camp are not drunkards.

2—Six hundred of us, men, women and children, live in 20-year-old wartime American Nissen huts. These huts were totally unfit for human habitation some ten years ago.

3—We appeal to you, our fellow-citizens, to help bring pressure on the housing authority, the Derry Corporation, to provide us with houses.

Time and again over a period of years, we have asked the Corporation to do this but without success.

4—We address this appeal to everybody, Members of Parliament, Aldermen and Councillors, Clergymen, Trade Unionists and Businessmen; to all those who are, or should be, concerned in conscience about the conditions under which we are forced to live.

Signed :

THE MEN, WOMEN AND CHILDREN, SPRINGTOWN CAMP.

JANUARY, 1964.

Pennyburn Youth Club in August 1988 on the 25th anniversary of Father Ferguson's ordination. Father Ferguson died in America a few years later in a motoring accident. Back: Kathleen McLaughlin, Sally Duffy, Roy McCallion, Collette Downey, Dorrie McKinney, Martin McLaughlin, Patsy Lynch, Collette Doherty, Ann Coyle, Roisin Rooney, Claire Duffy, Ella Ferguson and Moya Friel. Front: Thomas McCauley, Father Ferguson, Susan Lynch, Rosemary McColgan and Kathleen McGinty. (Courtesy Susan Lynch)

nil. Their situation changed after the residents mounted a campaign in 1964 and distributed leaflets calling for equality and fairness, which culminated in their marching to the Guildhall and taking over the mayor's parlour. The incident was widely publicised in the national media, and the disgraced and somewhat embarrassed Derry Corporation and County Councils were forced to alleviate the Springtown families' plight; the camp was finally closed in 1968.

Willie's Stowaway Rat

My wife's father, Willie Heaney, owned a small blue Ford van in which he delivered fresh vegetables; he also took his wife, Lizzie, shopping to the town in it two or three days a week. Another use for it was to carry small sacks of stale bread and meal for his four cows that he grazed in a field beside the Collon Lane just before Carnhill Estate was built.

On a few mornings when Willie opened the van door, he noticed pieces of the stale bread scattered over his driving seat and on the floor but never thought anything odd about it as he brushed the scraps off the seat. This kept re-occurring and Willie began to think Lizzie might be leaving the mess when taking some of the bread to feed the wild birds that flew into the front garden every day.

He thought nothing more about it until one day as he was parked in William Street, waiting for Lizzie to come out of McLaughlin's hardware shop where she went to purchase a new coal scuttle, he saw a huge grey rat sitting on the bonnet of his van. Willie watched it for a few moments as it sat on its hind legs, preening its muzzle and long black whiskers with its pink front feet, and then he tooted the horn, making the cheeky big rat scamper off in a flash.

The same thing happened a few more times when Willie parked in various places in the town and he began to wonder if the rodent had taken a liking to following him around just to sit on his vehicle, or did it do the same to other motorists? His family became used to hearing him and their mother relate their encounters with the rat and joked about it and named it Cousin Rasty. One day when Willie was driving to the field to feed his cows, he reached across to take his spare asthma inhaler from the glove compartment, when Cousin Rasty appeared as from nowhere and was sitting on the front passenger seat where Lizzie always sat on her trips to the town. He noticed it from the side of his eye, and the van screeched to a halt as a startled Willie forcefully applied the footbrake. Rasty made a rapid dash to his hideout or escape hole to avoid being shouted to death as Willie called all the unsavoury names he could think of after it.

It did the same on a number of other journeys over the next couple of weeks and Willie became convinced that the rat had taken up permanent abode somewhere inside the van. Each member of the Heaney family searched the vehicle thoroughly and his son Billy, who carried out all the maintenance, even jacked it up and took the wheels off to make a closer inspection on its underside and chassis but gave up the search, saying the animal must be living somewhere nearby. Then one day the van wouldn't start and Willie got Billy to look at the problem. Billy opened the bonnet and poked around the engine to discover that some of the wiring sheaths were frayed and ragged, which caused the bare wires to arc and disrupt the ignition connections. He put two and two together as he taped over the bared wiring and told his father that Cousin Rasty was the culprit; it had taken to gnawing through the wiring loom of the van and Billy warned that the vandal must be caught before the vehicle became a fire hazard.

An inch-by-inch search began of Willie's van, and every piece of stale bread, buckets, empty sacks, droving sticks, various tools, old overcoats, caps, scarves, gloves, wellington boots, pieces of rope and cord, long lost penknives, briar pipes and a whole lot of other comfooterments were piled against the garage wall. The van was swept clean of scurrying spiders and insects, along with the other bits of debris and dusty clay, until they were both satisfied that not another loose article or creature was left inside it.

As they stood pondering and looking into the spotlessly clean back of the van, they nearly jumped out of their skins when Rasty emerged from under the driving seat and scurried across the van floor to disappear under the passenger seat. Then they spotted it crawling up under the dashboard and, presumably, back to its hideout again. The engine compartment under the bonnet was searched and Cousin

Rasty's lodgings were discovered on top of a wheel arch. It was a thick comfortable nest, made from pieces of loom sheathing and bits of paper and rags. Lying in the middle of the nest was a litter of tiny, pink, hairless, helpless squirming creatures, waiting for their mother to supply their next meal that never came. The litter of rats was unceremoniously disposed of to the dustbin and a trap baited and laid to successfully put an end to Cousin Rasty's daily tours with Lizzie and Willie in his precious Ford van.

Snuff and Chewing Tobacco

Made from powdered tobacco by the two Irish tobacco companies, Gallaher and Grant, snuff was a very common addictive commodity used mainly by elderly women and a few men in Ireland for years up until the middle of the 1970s. It was sold in tobacconists and most corner shops, usually in quantities from a quarter-ounce to a pound (which was fourteen ounces), but most people purchased it in half-ounces; it was spooned into small cones made from paper, mostly pieces of newspaper. Some men and women kept it in small ornamented tins and silver snuff caskets with hinged lids that were sold in jewellers' shops, but most of the women I knew kept their snuff in little empty mustard-tin boxes.

Nearly every man, woman and child in Derry and Donegal had at one time or another sniffed a tiny pinch of snuff up their nostrils to enjoy the big sneeze that followed. That was how it was taken, and all over the town you could see little old ladies with brown upper lips and traces of snuff on the front of their blouses and coats. When ladies got together in a group, especially at wakes or weddings, or when visiting a mother with her new young baby, the snuff tins were passed around and each would take a small pinch between their thumb and forefinger, sniff it up her nose and then wipe her fingers on the front of her apron or dress; it didn't cause them to sneeze, because they were immune to its effects through years of snuffing. After a while, however, everybody else in the room, as well as the newly christened baby, would be sneezing. I'm sure that sometimes even in the wake house, the dead person's eyes were watering, the air was so filled with snuff.

I remember my father-in-law, Willie Heaney, woke up one morning to discover that his eye was swelled up like a golf ball and his eyelid wouldn't close over it. His son took him to the emergency clinic in Altnagelvin Hospital, where he went through a rigorous examination that lasted for over two hours by the baffled doctors, who finally, after many questions, found that the cause of the affliction was snuff that had fallen into his eye when Lizzie, his wife, had sat up in bed to have a sniff in the middle of the night. After getting his eye rinsed out and doctored, he recovered quickly and laughed about the incident when he went home.

Another unsavoury habit among men in those days was the chewing of tobacco. It was specially produced in a thin rope form that was bought by the half-ounce or ounce. In most public houses, spittoons for spitting into were placed near the counters and seating

Dan Hegarty taking a rest in Rose Griffin's Inishowen Bar, Rossville Street, in 1956.

areas, and I remember having to clean them out every morning when I was a teenager working in the Atlantic Bar in Foyle Street. They were still used in some bars until the late 1960s when I worked in the bottling stores. When a man chewed the tobacco at home, he spat into the open fire, and the hearth and surround would have had to be cleaned often by his mother or wife to get the big brown stains off them. It was a very unhygienic habit that unknowingly caused ill health to the many men who died of mouth and throat cancer through chewing tobacco over the years.

My grandfather chewed tobacco, and as he sat chewing in front of the fire one day, I watched him spitting into it. The family cat was sitting contently on the fender looking up at him, and some of the tobacco juice went into the poor creature's eye; it screeched with pain and ran up the walls and curtains and under the table and round the floor in circles. My father came into the room when he heard the commotion, and with his help, we managed to pin down the cat that was hissing and spitting at us. He poured cold water into its stinging eye before opening the back door to let it escape onto the roof of the coal shed to recover from its agonising ordeal.

Our First House and Home

Our second son, Billy, was born in February 1963 and christened in St Patrick's Church. The weather was very severe on the morning of the christening, with heavy drifts of snow that froze over on the roads and pavements, hampering the movement of traffic, which was light anyway in those days before the housing estates were built. The area was outside the city boundary and the Derry Corporation's control, which ended just above the church on the Buncrana Road, so the roads weren't treated with salt.

It was too dangerous to walk to the church to have the baby christened, and my wife and I were in a quandary whether to postpone the christening to some other day. Travelling by taxi wasn't a common mode of travel in Derry then – except for emergencies, weddings and funerals – because of the shortage of money.

Then a knock came to the back door and I opened it to find a near neighbour called Mickey McGuinness standing there in the falling snow. Mickey was one of the few people who owned a car, which he used to taxi in, and he said he had heard from my wife's mother that the baby was to be christened and had come to help us. No other traffic was on the Racecourse or Buncrana Roads that morning because of the weather, and Mickey took us, with God's help, slowly but safely to the church to get Billy christened as the car slid and slipped on its perilous journey.

Our living conditions with Rosita's grandparents were beginning to get very cramped. It became obvious that we needed more room, and

Pat and Mary Heaney with great-grandsons Patrick and Billy Cunningham, sitting in front of the fire-range in Oak Villa on the Racecourse Road in 1964.

although lucky and grateful enough to have somewhere to live, we tried unsuccessfully to find other accommodation. Due to the confined area of the small bedroom we slept in, which was situated directly over the living-room that was always overheated because of the constant use of the range, our baby Billy fell ill with pneumonia shortly after our Patrick suffered a collapsed lung. We were desperate to find a new permanent home and were constantly turned down by the Corporation and Housing Trust, which were responsible for building and allocating the houses. Many hundreds of other young families were worse off than us, and we would gladly have taken a hut in the Springtown Camp if any had been available.

A few months after the christening, my wife learned that she was going to have twins in March 1964, and we prayed that something would turn up; nothing did, and the twin boys, Philip and Joseph, were born. With not enough room for the six of us in the small bedroom, the two older boys were taken to Rosita's parents' house on the Buncrana Road to sleep with them every night. Then we heard from Rosita's father that one of his regular customers, by the name of Milligan, was selling her house in Mary Street and going to live in Portrush with her son Paddy, a well-known coach in the local boxing clubs who also took part in the annual sponsored walking races to raise money for charities in Derry.

After Mrs Milligan heard about our desperation for a house, she agreed to sell us hers for nine hundred pounds. We got a mortgage to repay at twelve pounds monthly, which was a huge undertaking for us then on account of the low wages that I earned and my wife not able to go to work. In those days, no family allowance money was given for a first child, but an allowance of half a crown was paid for the second and each subsequent child.

So, with the help of our friends and families giving us bits and pieces of second-hand furniture, and the generous financial aid from our parents to buy linoleum for the floors, we moved into our first home in Mary Street when the twin babies were six weeks old. My employer, Bobby Toland, also gave us some beautiful furniture that had been removed from his parents' vacated family home in Abercorn Road. At that time, second-hand household furniture was being shipped from Glasgow to the Derry quay, and I bought a double-sized bed from a dealer called Mickey McLaughlin who lived with his sister and brother-in-law, Johnny McDaid, in the Mourne Bar in Foyle Street. Pat Heaney, our milkman from Maybrook Dairy, and I collected the bed from the quay as it came off the Glasgow boat.

Mary Street, a cul-de-sac off Miller Street, is a terrace of thirteen houses with a row of houses facing them called Cooke Terrace. It was built in the 1890s and is one of a number of small streets set between Bishop Street and Foyle Road. Before we moved into the house, we cleaned it from top to bottom and painted and papered every room, including the tiny scullery that led to the backyard where the toilet and coalhouse were situated at the bottom of a flight of five steps outside the back door.

The lead gas and water pipes in the scullery were leaking and my father, who was a plumber/gas fitter, repaired them. The previous owner had the gas leak plugged with a piece of soap, which was a common way to temporarily stop a pin-sized gas leak in those days. The electric wiring was also in a dangerous state, with the socket for the smoothing iron mounted beside the window and connected from a light socket on the ceiling by a small adapter. I was repairing a loose wire in a bulb socket on the landing one day and accidentally shorted the fuse. This caused every house in the street to lose power because a main fuse had blown in the junction box situated at the bottom of the street. It needed the assistance of an engineer from the Electricity Department to solve the problem. The cause of the blackout was that a previous handyman had repaired a fuse wire in the house with a piece of tinfoil.

Every night before we retired to bed, my wife left out the butter in a dish, sugar in a bowl and a cup of milk on the table for me to use for my breakfast, because she lay on a while longer with the twins, Philip and Joseph, who kept us awake as we fed them during the night. I noticed on a few mornings some grains of sugar scattered on the table and marks on the butter, as well as drops of milk bedside the cup. Innocently, I thought that my eldest boy must have been out of his bed and helped himself to some food during the night and paid no more heed to it.

I was shaving at the kitchen sink before going out to work one morning and was planning to repair a few holes in the floor as I scraped the beard and foam from my chin. A worn-out piece of lino covered the uneven floor and I lifted one end of it with the toe of my boot to examine one of the holes; I froze when I saw two eyes looking up at me from within. Was it a mouse or a rat? I couldn't concentrate all that day in the bottling stores where I worked as I loaded and unloaded the delivery lorries and went about my other duties worrying about my wife and children in the house with vermin. I didn't tell my wife about the creature, as I didn't want to frighten her, and that evening, I purchased a box of rat poison and poured it down the hole next morning before going to work.

The author and his wife Rosita in their home in Mary Street in the early 1970s. Standing is Philip, and seated are Patrick, Gregory, Carol, Billy and Joseph.

Patrick and Billy Cunningham with their Granda Patrick in the backyard in Mary Street in 1964.

On returning home for my lunch break at one o'clock, I found Rosita huddling with the four babies in the front room where she had fled when she had heard the rats under the scullery floor squealing and scraping as they fought with each other to eat the poison. We got the babies ready and made our way by bus to her mother in Pennyburn, where they stayed for a few days while I, with the help of our friend Mickey Moore, who ran the local YP Hospitals Charity Pools office in Bishop Street, renewed the scullery floor with concrete.

That didn't end the rat problem, because they had been coming in under the scullery floor from a faulty outside drain and were now trapped under the wooden floor in the living-room. I discovered this, to my horror, on the first night my family returned and we were having our supper at bedtime. The floor began to vibrate as the rats started to gnaw their way through the wooden floor in the cubby-hole beneath the stairs. Luckily, I had procured three traps before the new floor was laid, and I set them under the stairs before we went to bed for a sleepless night. During the night, I heard one of the traps springing and went downstairs to investigate; I found two huge dead black rats stretched out in two of the traps.

The traps were set for another few nights, but there were no other rats under the floor, thanks be to God, and we were quite happy after I repaired the broken drain that led to the sewers in the yard. I told my neighbours about our ordeal and was surprised when five of them came to me, privately and unknown to each other, and asked me to deal with rats in their homes too. They had been too embarrassed to let anyone know they had vermin and I ended up fixing broken sewer pipes in all their yards as well.

Neighbourhood Shops and Pubs

At the bottom of Mary Street was Mrs McGrory's front-room shop that sold potatoes, bread, cigarettes, some confections, razor blades, babies' dummies, hairpins and other small household items. Mrs McGrory, who dressed in a long black dress and shawl, used a walking stick. At times, when she lost her patience with a child who took time to decide which sweets to buy, she slapped her stick on the counter to make the child hurry up. Adult customers and delivery men didn't escape her quick temper either and she was known to throw the stick or any other missile that came to hand at them if she mistakenly thought they were being cheeky towards her.

Her son, Pat, with his wife, Joan, and four sons and two daughters lived with her until they eventually moved into a house at the top of Cooke Terrace that was vacated by a family called Hutchinson, whose only two sons were policemen. When the decimal currency came into use in 1971, the children of the area were still using the old currency of pennies and ha'pennies for nearly six months afterwards to buy sweets in her shop. Even the bright pupils of nearby St Columb's College got wind the old lady in Mary Street was still dealing in the old money and descended in droves every lunchtime to buy their few cigarettes and sweets at half-price until she discovered that they were all taking advantage of her slowness in getting used to the new values of the decimal coinage.

The Parish Pastoral Centre at the corner of Miller Street and Bishop Street was formerly the boarding house for the pupils of St Columb's College, and once inside, after school was over, they had to obey the strict rules of staying indoors and had to obtain special permission to leave the building. I used to pity those from the outlying rural areas; they always had a hungry look about them and

Two excited boys looking at the toys displayed in the window of Edmiston's toyshop in Shipquay Street in the late 1950s.

I can imagine the hunger pangs they must have suffered when Mrs Duffy, whose chip shop was just a few yards away, began to fry her fish and chips in the evenings and the appetising smell of the hot cooking fat wafted in the breeze throughout the whole area, making both boarders and local residents water at the mouth.

At the junction of Bishop Street and Ferguson Street were Harry Grant's grocery store and Mrs Duffy's fish and chip shop. A few doors above Harry's shop was Grant's pork store, which employed twenty or thirty men dissecting and curing pig carcases; the firm moved to Culmore in the late 1960s.

Joe Gormley's small public house was next door to the Cairns family, and a few doors away was Joe Doherty's barber shop, where most of the men and boys had their haircuts and sometimes listened to Joe conversing in Gaelic with a customer. At the top of the street, near the junction of Abercorn Road, was Doherty's confectionery shop; the Dohertys moved in from Malin Head in the early '60s. At the junction of Bishop Street and Abercorn Road was the Horse Market Post Office. Across the street from Grant's were Jones and Lowther's Laundry and the Labour Exchange Bureau, otherwise called the 'brue', with the

A busy Bishop Street on a summer day during the second world war at the
junction of Barrack Street and Abercorn Road. (Courtesy E McDowell)

main entrance being in Barrack Street facing Gilmartin's bar and grocery store. Behind the laundry and brue was Corporation Street, where ABC Bakeries employed quite a number of men. When the bakery closed, it was taken over by the Atlantic Harvest fish processing company that was set up by Reggie Ryan and John Hume, who later went into politics and replaced Nationalist Eddie McAteer as an Independent Westminster MP for Derry.

The top end of Bishop Street above Abercorn Road was a busy place in the 1960s. The front gates of the Long Tower Boys' School, once the old Albert Market, were near a small shop commonly known as Wee Johnny's that sold and bought second-hand comic books as well as penny drinks of lemonade and sarsaparilla. Two brothers, Johnny and Bertie McLaughlin (who also lived there), owned the shop, where schoolboys passed enjoyable periods after school every day browsing through the comics while drinking their penny glasses of mineral waters. The more worldly-wise boys were allowed to play poker at the far end of the counter where Wee Johnny collected a percentage from each game's stake money. Beside Wee Johnny's was a fruit and vegetable shop owned by Louis O'Neill, whose two sons – John and Damien – were to become members of the famous Derry punk rock band, The Undertones. Along with fellow band members Fergal Sharkey, Billy Doherty and Michael Bradley, The Undertones often practised their music in a store at the back of O'Neill's shop.

There were six public houses between Bishop's Gate and the top of Abercorn Road, two of them owned by Benny Mullen: the Elephant Bar and the Arch Bar, which faced each other just outside of the gate; the Bell Bar, owned by Harry Doherty; and at the top of Henrietta Street, Mrs Bryson and her daughter, Betty, owned a little pub that had the strict rules of no singing or getting too drunk, and *definitely* no women to be served alcoholic beverages. It was a bar where men went to have a quiet chat and left to go home nearly sober when the bar closed at ten o'clock until six o'clock the next evening.

The stern, dark, grey structure of the Derry Jail that stood for one hundred and fifty years, with its battlemented towers looming starkly against the sky over the Fountain and surrounding areas, was the main feature at the top of Bishop Street. It closed in 1953 and was later used

The Undertones in the 1980s.

by the Civil Defence as a store and finally demolished in 1971 to allow the Fountain Estate to be built. Next to the jail, at the junction of Bennett Street and Bishop Street, was the Barrel Bar, owned by George Doherty. Many of the clientele came from the old Bridge Street and Orchard Street localities where George lived. The two O'Hara sisters had formerly owned the bar until the early '60s. A few of George's regular customers were teetotallers who didn't go there to drink but to take part in the darts matches and other social pastimes that gave the bar a pleasant atmosphere.

Beside the gates of the Long Tower Boys' School was the Brown Bear Bar, which was later renamed the Pop Inn, and owned by Jack Coyle, who once was a chemist in Campbell's pharmacy a few doors above the bar and also where Willie Temple from the Fountain began his apprenticeship in pharmacy. Mrs Barney McLaughlin and her daughter, Maureen, ran a bar nearby. Mrs Barney, as she was commonly known, also had a bar in Foyle Street. Tony O'Sullivan opened a public bar and lounge across the street in the late 1960s and named it Peyton Place after a popular weekly American TV soap programme of the same name. Other shops, a few doors above Peyton Place, were Paddy Ward's grocery and Denis Jackson's newspaper shop; Denis was also an agent for Littlewood's and Vernon's pools. Billy Melaugh, who worked there for a number of years, eventually became the owner after Denis retired.

At the top of Bishop Street, near the gate, were quite a number of shops, including John McHugh's general groceries and provisions; a barrel of salted herrings stood outside the shop door and all the children who passed by had a long look into the barrel to examine the cured fish that had their eyes and mouths wide open as well as their own. Arthur Breslin's fruit and vegetable shop, Hippsley's vegetable and confectionery shop and Mark McChrystal's paint and wallpaper shop all faced Barr's pawnshop and Willie Carlin's 'Bazar' (the sign writer left out an 'a' when he painted it). (Willie's brother, James, was the proprietor of the Cosy Inn Bar at the bottom of Church Brae in Drumahoe.) A pet shop was beside the Arch Bar and Colhoun's Bakery at the entrance to the Fountain area, and below the bakery were the All Cash Stores and Fiorentini's fish and chip shop.

Left: Bill Hipplsey at the front door of his shop at 57 Bishop Street in 1969. Above: Bessie Hippsley relaxing at home, 1999. (Courtesy Sandra Doherty, née Hippsley)

Arthur Breslin, grandfather of well-known Derry musicians Declan and Tony Carlin, taking a breath of fresh air in the doorway of his fruit and vegetable shop at 39 Bishop Street in the early 1930s. Note the two bunches of rhubarb hanging on the wall beside the window. (Courtesy Fionnuala Carlin)

Facing the Derry Jail, Duffy's cattle dealers had a huge open area at the back of the shops where at times they kept up to 300 cattle before taking them to the market. Nearby was McLaughlin's workshop where coffins were made for the local undertakers, and as you passed by, you could hear the eerie sounds of the hammering of nails and clinking of the brass handles and name-plates being sorted out to be fixed onto the coffins. At the junction of Henrietta Street and Bishop Street was a dry-cleaning laundry. Those were the more popular establishments at the top of the street and now and then small shops were opening for short periods before closing and moving on to other areas.

Between the top of Miller Street and the bottom of Bishop Street at Foyle Road were five public houses: Jim and Peggy O'Hara's, once owned by Mulherns; Mickey Lynch's at the top of Brook Street; and Eddie Doherty's at the junction of Foyle Road. On the other side was Hugh and Agnes McAnee's Silver Dog, and at the end of a row of eight houses called Fitter's Row was the First and Last Bar – the name denoting it was the first bar to be encountered on entering Derry from the Letterkenny direction and the last bar when leaving the city. Bars belonging to Derry City football club and the BOC (British Oxygen Company) opened at the end of the 1960s as social clubs.

Most of the bars in Derry strictly obeyed the official opening times, ie 10.00am to 10.00pm, but some of them were lax in observing the law by allowing patrons to stay on the premises until after midnight as long as they remained quiet when the RUC were about.

On Sunday mornings, it wasn't unusual to see men tapping on the bar doors and slipping inside to have a drink or a cure when it opened slightly, and if there was access from a rear lane to the bar, it was safer to slip in through the back door.

Peggy and Jim O'Hara lived across the street from their bar, which they didn't open until eleven o'clock at night for late drinkers, some of whom had just left the other early-closing ones. It used to be quite a novelty to sit in the friendly company of them both as they light-heartedly bantered each other and took part in the lively conversations with the late-night drinkers. Little did the happy couple know then the heartache in store for them when their son, Patsy, would die on hunger strike in Long Kesh prison camp in June 1981.

Jim O'Hara carrying his son Patsy's coffin. Beside Jim is his wife Peggy along with some of their family in 1981.

Shops in the lower end of Bishop Street were: McMenamin's All Cash Stores at the top of Miller Street (later run by Speedy McGilloway); Ricky and Lena Phelan's confectionery store; a shoe shop in Archie Adams's house, run by Mr McGlinchey; and below the Silver Dog Bar was Kitty Barratt's grocery shop. In Fitter's Row, which was the last row of houses at the bottom, was a small front-room-parlour shop that sold sweeties and cigarettes.

Unfortunate Winos

There, but for the grace of God, go I. A phrase often used by Derry people when expressing pity for those experiencing difficulties with alcohol or other addictions.

Alcoholism wasn't a big talking point in the 1950/60s, and many Derry people hardly even knew what the word meant, because only a small number of unemployed men were regularly seen about the town drunk. They were, as we would know now, alcoholics but were referred to as winos because they inevitably ended up drinking the cheapest alcohol available at that time, ie VP British wine which was a mixture of industrial alcohol and grape juice. It is ironic that nowadays, drinking wine is associated with a more affluent lifestyle.

Those men who suffered from the problem didn't pester anybody, but were willing to oblige people by doing small light jobs for them in return for a few shillings to buy some drink. Those unfortunate characters had often once been in the army or had emigrated and tramped through England and Scotland in their younger days looking for work until homesickness made them return to their native Derry to sign on the dole. Many others never came back at all and were lost forever to their home and families.

Winos in the 1950s and '60s suffered extreme hardships without the government financial assistance or charitable institutions that exist today to help them. They had several methods of obtaining alcohol, one of them being to go into one of the railway goods' yards where the empty whiskey barrels were kept in readiness for transport to the distillers in the south of Ireland. They boiled a kettle of water and poured it into a barrel and shook it about until the hot water washed the whiskey out of every seam and grain of the staves inside the barrel. The barrel was then drained out into the kettle and the whiskey-flavoured liquid shared out between them. Another way of getting alcohol was to melt some shoe polish in a large spoon over a flame and drain the spirit off into a cup. The same method was used to extract the spirit from Brasso, a liquid polish that housewives used for cleaning and shining brass.

White methylated spirits could only be bought in a chemist's shop, and some winos gave young boys a penny each for purchasing it for them, because the chemist wouldn't serve it to the winos, knowing they were going to drink it and cause damage to their livers. I remember working as an apprentice in the Atlantic Bar in Foyle Street when a wino came in to use the toilet. After he left, I was sent to see that everything was in order, and, finding a heavy obnoxious smell coming from the urinals so overpowering, I had to hold my breath until I got out into the bar area again to fetch the barman, Hugh Rooney. When he smelt it, he told me that the man who had just left had been drinking meths, and the only way to rid the heavy odour from the

Eddie 'Tipperary' Canavan, Andy Hegarty and Eddie 'Gacka-Wacka' McLaughlin in the background taking shelter from the rain in a vacant house in Fahan Street in the 1960s. (Courtesy Hugh 'Badger' McDaid)

place was to wave a lighted, rolled-up newspaper around to burn away the smell as well as fumigating the place with the smoke.

Eddie 'Tipperary' Canavan was a popular character from Springtown Camp, and each day he would come into the town and greet everyone he met with a smile and say, 'Aye-aye, captain.' Tipp, as he was referred to, was unemployed but was willing to run errands for the shop owners around William Street and Lecky Road and was repaid with either cash or cigarettes or some food. He and his companions were never turned away from Doherty's bakery shop and café in William Street, where they were given a breakfast at any time of the day.

A few of those men who tramped the streets of Derry for years, and slept out in the open on many wet and cold nights, became strict teetotallers in their thirties and carried out voluntary work for years afterwards, helping other unfortunate men and women to find comfortable shelter and care, care that would not become available for many years from some established charitable organisations such as the St Vincent de Paul Society in the town.

An amusing story by one of them, Tom (not his real name), told about one late evening when himself and Tipperary Canavan (who were close drinking friends) were making their way back to their respective places of abode for the night along Rossville Street after hanging about the streets and bars of Derry. As they parted at the bottom of Fahan Street, where Tom was about to begin his journey up the steep banking to his home in Walker's Place, he said to Tipperary, 'I'll give you a knock in the morning.'

Tipp answered, 'You'll need to bring a door with you, Tom.'

'Why's that, Tipp?' he asked.

'Because I'll be sleeping out on the bankin' tonight,' answered Tipperary as he went on his way.

Eddie 'Gacka-Wacka' McLaughlin from the Waterside and Paddy 'Neck' O'Neill, who lived near the bottom of Bishop Street, were two other harmless winos who were courteous to everybody they came in contact with, as were all of those men of that era. Not so in these early years of the third millennium, when addicts and drunks as young as ten years old are roaming the streets at all hours of the night causing harm to themselves and other innocent people they happen to come across. It would seem that at present they have been abandoned to their fates by some of the city's publicans, off-licence proprietors and town elders.

Two brothers nicknamed 'Gander' and 'Spider' Scanlon, who had been in the army in their younger days, were winos who did menial work to earn enough money to feed their habits. In 1969, Mickey Carlin and I found Spider lying in the gutter at the top of Long Tower Street near Bishop's Gate one evening as we were coming from work and carried him onto the footpath to sit him against Arthur's pawnshop wall. A passing army patrol radioed for an ambulance to give him some medical assistance. But Spider was past needing help; he was

A British Army squaddie clasping the hand of an embarrassed Paddy 'Neck' O'Neil on Bishop Street at the top of Long Tower Street in 1969. (Courtesy Fr Frank Deeney)

Tony 'Tight' Downey singing to the passers-by in Waterloo Square in 2004.

Bosco Hegarty in his usual happy mood enjoying a pint in Badger's Bar. (Courtesy Hugh 'Badger' McDaid)

dead. Finding Spider like that saddened me for a long while after. To think that here was a man who had played happily as a child in Long Tower Street and died a lonely man in the gutter.

Spider earned his nickname from the boxing skills he acquired while being in the army, the same name as was given to Derry's famous Spider Kellys, Jimmy and Billy, the first father and son to win the British and European bantamweight crown and who received little or no acknowledgement for that unique achievement from the higher boxing echelons or top sports writers.

Dan Gallagher, father of world-famous guitarist and singer-songwriter Rory Gallagher, was another unfortunate with a drinking problem. I remember Dan trying to sell records of his son to the young people around Orchard Row where he lived and they not believing he was Rory's father and making fun of him. Rory at the time lived in Cork along with his mother and the rest of his family.

Sheila Brennan and Sammy Wray were a couple dedicated to each other and could always be seen in the vicinity of lower William Street and Waterloo Street in all kinds of weather during the 1970s and '80s. They were given meals every day in Frankie Ramsey's and Doherty's cafés. Derry folks, who fondly tolerated their seemingly unending intoxicated state, showed a lot of sympathy and Christianity towards them because of their poor social and health conditions.

Maggie MacKay

Maggie MacKay was a local character who frequented the lower William Street and Strand Road areas of Derry in the 1940s and '50s. She dressed in a long black dress and wore a black woollen shawl about her head and shoulders.

Maggie was fond of a little drop of drink and a nice wee sailor now and then, and one night, the local policeman on his beat came across her standing in the shadows in the cross lanes at the bottom of William Street with the front of her dress up over her face and head. When the policeman put her dress into a more modest position, he found that she was eating a bag of chips. Maggie was very startled on seeing the policeman and inquired in a surprised tone, 'Has the wee sailor gone?'

On the odd occasion, Maggie, for some minor offence, was put into the Strand Road police cells for the night, more to give her a warm place to sleep than for punishment. Once, she was asked by one of the local women if she liked being in jail and answered that she liked the jail but didn't like the people in there.

Maggie went into the Long Tower Church one afternoon to pray to Mary and request her help in recovering the five pounds that she foolishly had put on a losing bet in McColumb's bookies shop. She knelt in a front-row seat, facing the life-size statue of Our Lady that stood at the left-hand side of the high altar, praying in a loud voice as if she were having a normal conversation. 'It was supposed to be a sure winner, Mary, and I was silly enough to listen to auld Paddy Strain. He told me that he was just after getting the tip from the horse's mouth. Sure he must have got it from its arse, because now I know that he was talking a load of sh***!'

As Maggie was telling the statue how the race went and about her horse finishing second last, Paddy Cleary, the church sacristan, who happened to be working behind the statue of Our Lord on the opposite side of the altar, was listening to her. He kept from her view and thought he would play a prank on Maggie by addressing her from his hiding place, hoping she would think that God was speaking to her. 'Go on home, Maggie,' he said in his deepest and gentlest voice, 'and don't be so foolish with your money again. Just offer up your lost five pounds to the saints in Heaven.'

Maggie glowered under her brow, turned her head towards the 'speaking' statue of Our Lord and scowled, 'Mind your own business, You, and have a bit of manners when I'm talking to your mother.'

People and Places

Our fifth son, Gregory, was born in May 1965, just fourteen months after the twins, Philip and Joseph. Carol, our only daughter, was born three years later in November 1968. Our sixth and last son, Edward, waited until December 1977 to join the family, and we named him after our newly ordained bishop, Edward Daly.

Our young family took up all of our time as we lovingly cared for them. We took them out every day when the weather was dry, and on Sundays our favourite place was 'out the line', the commonly used name of the walk along the old, disused GNR railway line that ran parallel with the River Foyle. We often met many other newly married couples who were also with their own young families, and we watched men and boys fishing for trout or walking their dogs and making them retrieve sticks from the river. The line was a beautiful place to spend an evening in the good weather, with its many trees and bushes lining the route out past the 'secret passages', Anthony's Rock, the green beds and finally, to our usual destination of Moore's Quay, where the children often paddled barefoot in the cool waters of the Foyle that lapped on its shingled shore.

Former British and Empire boxing champion Billy 'Spider' Kelly giving Joe McGowan a couple of self-defence tips in Waterloo Place in June 2004.

Skinny dippers learning to swim in the River Foyle out the line at
Letterkenny Road in the early 1950s.

The more daring older boys and young men from the Brandywell
and Bishop Street areas swam in the river and we would often watch
some of the more experienced swimmers, including my cousin Willie
Cooley, swimming to the other side and resting a while on the far shore
at Prehen before venturing back. The swimmers may not have known
then that the River Foyle is second only to the Rhine as the fastest
flowing river in Europe, but they knew the tide wasn't in full flow and
would have been more dangerous when at its fastest ebb.

I saved one pound every week in the Derry Credit Union in the
Rossville Hall and got a loan every year to take the family for two weeks
holidays in Buncrana. Not owning a car, my workmate in the bottling
stores, Brian McChrystal, took us there in the work's van, and it was
loaded with all the children's clothes, which included raincoats, hats,
wellington boots and warm jumpers, along with two cots, a large pram,
footballs, buckets and spades, tins of beans and packets of cornflakes
and everything else that we would need for the fortnight. When the
van was loaded, the older boys sat in the back on top of the boxes of
stuff, and my wife and me and two babies in the front seat beside
Brian. We were the happiest family in Derry as we drove down the road

to our favourite holiday resort. Hail, rain or shine, we went to the shore every day and took lots of sandwiches and bottles of water and milk with us. At the end of our holidays, everything was packed into the van again, and with glum faces, we went back home to Derry and our overcrowded drab street again.

St Columba's Church was commonly referred to as the Long Tower, and we took the children there every Sunday and holy day when they were old enough to go to school. Father McGaughey was the CC, and Fathers Rafferty and Carlin were new to the parish. It was the church where I was christened and attended with the rest of my family when I lived as a boy in Friel's Terrace at the back of the Walls. I met many of my old neighbours who still lived in Nailor's Row and Walker's Place every Sunday, and frequently during the week, until they were all re-housed in the late '60s and early '70s when the redevelopment of the Bogside and surrounding areas was taking place. Many residents from Walker's Place and Nailor's Row were re-housed in the Creggan and Shantallow Estates, and most of the people in Friel's Terrace moved to the high flats in Rossville Street.

My cousin Willie Cooley and his family, who had lived in our old home ever since we left in 1950, were the last to leave the back of the Walls in 1972 and went to live in Lisfannon Park in the Bogside. I still have many happy memories of growing up at the back of the Walls and its lovely characters and people: Con Bonnar and his wife Sally in Walker's Square; Paddy and Maggie Strain, who lived two doors away from us; Annie Barr's lodging house at the top of the street and all the men who had stayed there over the years; Bobby Piggott from Howard Street; Danny Feeney, who once drove the horse-drawn hearse for McGaughey's Funeral Undertakers; Andy and Bosco Hegarty; Bella 'Butts' Doherty, who sold the ha'penny plates of peas and beans in her front room; the Scanlon brothers, Gander and Spider; Ducky Carlin, who went to the Gasyard and carried bags of coke on his back every week to his elderly neighbours; Paddy Deane, who was reputed to be the tallest man in Derry; and Wee Johnny Nichol from Nelson Street, who spent a few hours every day on Derry's Walls looking through the portholes at everything below in our street and in the Bogside. The children of the area believed that Wee Johnny, who always had his hands

St Columba's Church Long Tower Choir on its annual outing to the Northern Star Hotel, Dunfanaghy, in the 1950s. Back L to R: Paddy Cleery, P Devine, Gerry McCarron, Danny Lynch, Alex Boyle, Hugh McDaid, Dan McConnologue, Seamus Browne, Alan Fox and Jan Molloy. Middle L to R: Paddy Walker, Barry Kelly, Paddy Hutton, Unknown, Pete Kyle, Willie Conaghan, Da Doherty, Michael Mason, Owen McKee, Robby Lewis and Neil Carlin. Front L to R: Eddie O'Neil, Mickey Carlin, Willie Cooley, Frannie O'Hara, Raymond Power, Hugh McCafferty and Bobby O'Donnell. (Courtesy P O'Neil)

Long Tower parishioners praying at Our Lady of Lourdes Grotto in the Brandywell on the Feast of the Immaculate Conception on a wet December evening in 1963. (Courtesy P O'Neil)

Above: Children in Nailor's Row in the 1950s posing with two bicycles, one with no wheels and the other with no handlebars. No expensive toys in those days. Pictured are Daniel Cullen, Mark McGlinchey, Frankie McGlinchey and Charlie McGlinchey. The little boy is Pat Cooley. (Courtesy Margaret McGlinchey)

Left: Paddy Deane, reputed to be the tallest man in Derry in his youth, resting on his windowsill in Nailor's Row in the 1940s. (Courtesy Margaret McGlinchey, née Deane)

up his coat sleeves behind his back, carried a knife and was waiting for someone to pounce on; of course that was only a story made up by our parents in order to frighten us if we misbehaved.

An amusing but dangerous incident happened in Walker's Place when a row of old, crumbling houses at the top of the banking had to be evacuated; some of them were falling into the banking while the people were still living there in the early 1950s. One male resident was still asleep in his bed one evening in Walker's Square after drinking a bottle of wine as the demolition squad tumbled the house next door. He was wakened by the noise and his bed rocking about when the bedroom swayed to and fro and the wall fell out into the street. He sat on the edge of his bed and looked down into the road where the workmen were staring up at him and their mouths hanging open at the sight of him; they had thought all the houses in the street were empty.

Paddy Quinn and Paddy O'Neil standing at the top of the banking in Walker's Square in the late 1950s. (Courtesy Paddy O'Neil)

Above: Sunning themselves after coming from the annual Retreat in the Long Tower Church in Walker's Square in the 1950s are: Jack Roper, Patsy 'Snipe' Hegarty, Paddy O'Donnell and Ming Harkin. (Courtesy Paddy O'Neil)

Left: Ellen Hutton, née O'Neil, with baby Cathleen in her arms outside her home in Walker's Square in the early 1960s. Includes back: Donal Cullen, Ann Bonnar, P Green and Jean Nash. Front: M Cullen, Margaret Hutton, McGuinness, Marie Hutton and McGuinness. (Courtesy Paddy O'Neil)

The resident sobered up in an instant and made a hasty exit to the safety of the street to let the gang continue with their task of demolishing the last of the old, crumbling houses at the top of the banking in the Square. A row of younger houses on the opposite side of the street were eventually tumbled a few years later in the 1960s.

Lundy's Day in Derryspeak

Here's an example of the Derry English we spoke when I lived as a boy outside the western side of Derry's Walls beneath the shadow of Governor Walker's monument and overlooking the Bogside. It is a true incident that happened to my brother and me one Lundy's day (18 December) in 1942 when we were very young.

> *Wan Lundy's day, me broller an me ris early. Me da wuz gittin ready tae go tae work in the gashyard. Ee wuz bittin' eez aig an milk up in a boul wae a fork tae mik scrammelled aigs fur eez brekfast. We wur jist sittin' on the fire fender in wur shurt tails, an me ma called down from the bedroom tae 'im, 'Wud ye mick a tist o brochan fur the wains an then give thim a drop o tae an a piece an jam before ye gout tae work?'*
>
> *Wur ganseys wur hingin' over a chair an wur polished brogues under the tibble, but instead of puttin' thim on, we ran outy the dure inty the street in wur bare feet. We ran down tae the bottim o' the street and stopped tae luck up at Derry Walls tae see Lundy the Tritter hingin' on Governor Walker's pillar wur ee wuz goney be burned litter on that day wae the Apprentice Boys o' Derry. He had on eez admiral's hat an a long coat, an had a bunnel o' sticks on eez back. As we wur luckin' up at eez big black boots an callin', 'Lundy the tritter, the big belly blither, ee cleaned eez arse wae a wee bit of pipper,' ee swung round wae the wund.*
>
> *Then a voice shouted down at us, 'Git away on up tae the house wae yeese an git on your shoes or yeese ill git a founderin.' It scarred the life outy us an we ran back inty the house an toul*

wur da what Lundy the Tritter siz tae us. Wur da siz that it wuz eez ghost back luckin' fur the keys o' the gits o' Derry that ee sould fir a bap durin' the siege o' Derry in 1689, an that ee had no bisness chissin' me an me broller up home.

That evnin', whin Lundy wuz bleezin' an cracklin' in the dark, a woman came out wae a big boccle o' holy water an sprinkled it over iverywan. No-wan evin thought of sendin' fur the farmagade in kiss eez sparks fell ontae our houses an set thim on fire. Whiniver Lundy the Tritter wus burnin', iverywan in the street burned thur chimleys too, so that the smoke from thim blew up ontae the Walls tae choke ivrybody on thim. Most times the smoke blew the wrong way an we wur choked wursells.

The nixt week, the pleece came roun wur houses an fined ivrywan sixpence fir mickin' more smoke than Lundy the Tritter.

Con Bonnar with his wife Sally kneeling bedside a grotto in Walker's Place in the 1940s. (Courtesy Paddy O'Neil)

Residents from Walker's Square in the early 1960s. Includes: Nina Hutton, Ella Quinn, Margaret Browne (née Bonnar), Lily Bonnar and Joe Browne. (Courtesy Paddy O'Neil)

Pounds From Heaven

Lizzie McGarrigle, one of Paddy Strain's daughters, told me many yarns about her father over the years that I've known her. The following, with Lizzie's kind permission, is one that I have put a little exaggeration to.

Nailor's Row was a long, narrow street of fifty-nine small two-up and two-down terraced houses, built in the latter part of the nineteenth century and demolished by the end of 1973. The Row perched on the top of a steep grassy embankment that overlooked the maze of similar-type streets that was Derry's Bogside.

Paddy 'Peggy' Strain lived in number 23 Nailor's Row with his wife Maggie and their family of five boys and four girls. He was a tall, blond-haired man with broad shoulders and lean muscular frame and had a pleasant, friendly face with pale blue eyes that always had a childish, mischievous expression about them. Maggie, a woman of average height and straight, shoulder-length black hair that had many

Above: Paddy 'Peggy' Strain standing at the bottom of Friel's Terrace in Nailor's Row in 1969. (Courtesy Fr Frank Deeney)

Left: Lizzie McGarrigle, a daughter of Peggy Strain, cutting the cloth to make patchwork quilts in the Pilot's Row Centre.

Derry dockers in the hold of a coal boat grafting hard for their living in 1969.
(Courtesy Fr Frank Deeney)

streaks of grey running through it, showed, in her shape, the results of having borne a lot of babies (some of them stillborn) in her first fifteen years of marriage and living in extreme poverty. The cares of her world showed through her smile when she greeted anyone on her way to the local grocery shop and to Mass on Sunday mornings. Paddy worked at the Derry docks, which wasn't a lucrative means of earning a living in the 1940s, especially not for him, who was very fond of the drink. Suffice to say, the Strains weren't too well off and Maggie was always in debt, finding it extremely difficult to make ends meet with little or no money being given to her by Paddy, who would rather spend most of it in Tracy's public house where many other men who worked at the quay spent their hard-earned wages as well.

Father Monagle, the small, stockily built priest in charge of St Columba's Church, was doing some of his frequent home visits in the street and dropped in to see Maggie, who sat at a bare table, breastfeeding her youngest baby of four months. Paddy was asleep on the hard, wooden sofa in the living-room, a thin stream of brown porter-coloured spittle trickling from the corner of his open mouth and dripping onto the collar of his open-necked shirt. On hearing about her plight, and seeing the poverty she and the children had to endure, the priest shook Paddy awake by pushing an open hand against his shoulder. He jumped to his feet, roaring like a stabbed bull until he saw that it was a priest confronting him. Father Monagle cowed him by making the sign of the cross with his hand towards Paddy and sat down beside him on the sofa, where he talked gently to him and Maggie about the evils of overindulging in the Devil's buttermilk, which in turn led men to neglect their families.

The priest left the house, with Paddy promising to take the pledge the next day. True to his word, he did, and for the following few weeks, the Strains' home became a happier one, with some of the older children getting new clothes, their old ones being handed down to the next in line. Maggie even bought herself a new flowered pinafore and paisley-decorated headscarf. She thought about the time only a year before when she had taken Paddy's suit to the pawnshop and pledged

Willie 'Da' Devlin unloading coal at the Derry Quay in 1970.
(Courtesy Fr Frank Deeney)

it for ten shillings. When Paddy went to change into it that evening to go and drink at the dockers' annual Christmas party in Tracy's bar, he found out what she had done. He screamed blue murder and put on one of Maggie's old frocks and sat on a chair outside his front door to embarrass her and the whole family. *Please God, he will stay away from the pub for good*, she thought. But it was only wishful thinking, because men like Paddy don't change their lifelong habits so easily, a lesson that Maggie had learnt so many distressing times before.

One Friday evening after eating his dinner of boiled potatoes and fried herrings, Paddy sat on a low wooden stool in front of the open fire. He was shifting about, very restless, and now and then wiped the back of his hand along his lips and then licked his lips again as if he was wiping and licking off the creamy white foam that used to deposit there after taking a long, cool, smooth drink of velvety black porter, which once was his favourite drink in Tracy's pub those long, long five weeks ago. He missed the craic and the banter with the other men in the bar and imagined that he could now hear the till bell ringing amidst the laughter and the smells of the tobacco smoke and pleasant aromas of the beers and porter and the urine-scented draught from the toilet, all mingling together in the bar, dulling the never-ending pains and miseries of the harsh world that existed outside the happy, homely, friendly public house at the bottom of Waterloo Street.

The urge for one last drink with his old drinking pals was gnawing at the taste buds in the most tender areas inside his mouth, which kept filling up with sweet saliva that he had to swallow in order that it wouldn't spill over to run down his chin. The more he craved a drink, the more his mouth watered. Paddy's willpower gradually weakened, until it finally snapped and he rose from the chair to go out of the house. While lifting the latch of the front door, he put his hand into his pocket and, finding it empty, remembered that for the past five weeks he had been handing all his earnings to Maggie, in keeping with his promise to Father Monagle to stay off alcohol and be more generous to his wife and children.

He returned to the living-room and asked Maggie if she had any money left and if she would give him a pound or two to pay off some of his outstanding debts in Tracy's Bar. Maggie replied that she had no money left to give him after paying off some of her own debts and the weekly housekeeping bills. She knew from previous painful experiences that Paddy's craving for the cursed drink had begun to work on him again at the end of a very restful and contented five weeks for her and the family. Now the worries and hunger and sadness for her wains would return to her home again as her husband would become the 'house devil' and 'street angel' again.

On being told there was not a penny in the house, Paddy became alarmed and felt like a trapped animal as he paced up and down the room, wringing his hands and wiping his mouth now and then between his forefinger and thumb to dry the fluid that bubbled out from the corners of his lower lip. The craving was welling up inside him and he felt an anger building up inside his head and chest towards his wife and spoilt brats of wains, and all of his and her relations, and the whole damned street full of rotten bastards, and all of the goody-goody people who over the past five weeks greeted him and told him, 'You're doing great, Paddy, and keep it up, because you and Maggie are like a newly wedded couple again.'

'To hell with the lot of you,' he muttered out loud as he stood in front of the picture that hung on the wall above the mantelpiece over the fire. It was an image that was common in every Catholic home in Ireland – the Sacred Heart of Jesus with the flaming heart of love for all mankind, showing the upturned palms of His bleeding hands.

Jesus seemed to be looking into Paddy's eyes as Paddy stared into His, and Paddy pleaded with Him to please help him to escape from this torment and to send him down a pound or two or else he would wreck the house. Paddy reached over the mantelpiece to straighten up the picture so that he could look straight into God's all-seeing eyes. And when he did so, to his astonishment, three one-pound notes fell down onto the mantelpiece from behind the picture. He crossed himself with the moneyed hand and thanked God and His Blessed Mother, Mary, for performing the miracle.

Without speaking to Maggie, who sat staring at the Sacred Heart picture and then at him, he made a beeline to the front door and slammed it behind him on his way out to the pub. Paddy Strain's five weeks of pretending to be a home-loving family man were over until

Father Monagle's next annual house visits in Nailor's Row.

Maggie Strain, with big tears of disappointment and desperation rolling down her cheeks, rose slowly from the empty table and placed her baby into its Moses basket. She began wringing her hands before clasping them tightly against her bosom and crossed the room to stand in front of the fireplace to look up into the Sacred Heart's innocent countenance. 'Sweet Heart of Jesus, why did you give him my meagre savings?' she pleadingly asked. 'You knew that was the only money I have ever managed to scrape together since the day I married that drunkard, and it was to buy myself a new pair of shoes to replace these old battered-out things I have on my feet for the past two years, and them packed with cardboard to keep out the water on wet days,' her tones getting louder and more aggressive.

She was angry now and slapped the front of the picture with the palm of her hand as if to punish God for giving in to her selfish husband. When she struck the Sacred Heart picture, the cord broke and the picture fell and landed on one of its corners on top of the mantelpiece. Maggie's heart seemed to miss a beat or two with horror as she tried to catch the picture just as it bounced off the mantelpiece shelf and hit the iron fire-fender where the glass smashed into jagged bits and pieces and its gold-painted frame broke away at the corners.

All of the wains, on hearing the crash, ran into the living-room to gather around their mother, who was shaking with fear after causing the precious picture of the Sacred Heart of Jesus to fall from its place of worship. Maggie asked God for forgiveness for her anger and selfishness by hiding money from her husband. The only things salvaged were the picture and its stiff cardboard backing as Maggie and her eldest daughter brushed up the fragments of glass and broken frame.

The picture, still loosely stuck to its cardboard backing, was now propped up on the mantelpiece as Maggie and her children knelt on the floor in front of it, saying prayers for their daddy and all their relations, and for all the poor black babies in Africa and all of the souls in purgatory, and for Father Monagle who had to collect money to give to the poor and send to the black babies' mothers, and maybe someday he might give them a few shillings, too. As they were finishing saying a Hail Mary, they heard the front door open and footsteps shuffling in the hallway. All heads turned towards the living-room door to see who was coming in. They could hear friendly low voices on the other side, which got more distinguishable as the door opened wider, and into the room stepped Father Monagle along with Paddy. Both were smiling, and the priest told them to keep kneeling and he would bless them all where they were.

When they were on their feet again, Maggie asked if there was anything wrong, and Father Monagle then told her that he had met Paddy walking down Waterloo Street and asked him how he was getting along, because he knew just how much of a struggle people like Paddy went through to overcome their addictions. After talking with Paddy the whole way down to the bottom of the street, they stood talking another while outside Tracy's public house, where three drunks emerged swearing at each other and at passers-by, one of them even urinating against the wall. Paddy told Father Monagle that the three men were his old drinking pals and that he was on his way to join them when he happened to meet him at the top of the street. On seeing the state his friends were in, Paddy realised that he was no stranger to that same scene they now were watching, because he was always among them. 'He asked me to walk along with him back to your house and have a drop of tea. So here we are, Maggie,' explained the priest.

She then told Father Monagle the whole story about her hidden money dropping from behind the picture, about her falling out with the Sacred Heart of Jesus and hitting and knocking the picture to the ground, and would Father Monagle say a wee prayer that everything gets all right again. He said he would, then put on a stern face as he reached up to lift the picture from the mantelpiece to see if there were any scratches on it. On inspecting it, he pulled the picture away from its cardboard backing, and two pieces of paper seemed to fall out and float to the floor. They lay there for five or ten seconds before the wide-eyed spectators recognised them as five-pound notes, and them as clean and crisp as the day they came from the royal mint. Maggie blessed herself with the sign of the cross as she said in a soft voice, 'Jesus, Mary and Joseph, it's a real miracle this time,' remembering how Paddy believed that he had witnessed one when her three pounds fell from behind the picture just an hour earlier.

The 1947 Sisters of Mercy Convent School Feis choir in Artillery Street. Back row: Rose McAnaney, Ethna Roberts, Molly O'Brien, Eileen Doherty, Rachael McCartney, Celine McKinney, Tess McColgan, Maureen McManus, Francis McSherry, Nellie O'Hagan and Martha Clifford. Middle row: Stephanie Crumlish, Lily Monteith, Collette Scanlon, Mary Browne, Sadie McIntyre, May McLaughlin, Sheila Doherty, Jean Lynch and Susie Cunningham. Front Row: Celia McReynolds, Ita McLaughlin, Jane Smith, Bernie Mullan, Teresa Kavanagh, Lila Clarke, Teresa Fisher, Anne Roddy, Kathleen McAllister, Roseanne McGowan, Chris McManus and Pearl Harrigan. (Courtesy Jean McCallion)

Father Monagle lifted the money from the floor and handed it to Maggie, who kissed it and said, 'Thanks, Father, and Glory be to God for this happy evening.' At that moment, Paddy, who was standing silently, gobsmacked, put his hand into his pocket and reached three crumpled notes to his wife as the wains began to chatter and laugh about the strange, exciting scenes they were witnessing in the middle of the living-room.

After all the pleasant excitement and commotion had settled down, the three adults had a well-deserved cup of tea and the children shared a bag of chips, bought out of one of the fivers, from Dan McGilloway's chip shop at the top of the street. Just before Father Monagle made his leave, he blessed the now happily united family from the living-room door before going into the street to make his way back to his parochial house.

Anyone who might have watched him that particular evening would not have failed to see a mischievous twinkle in Father Monagle's eyes and hear him hum a little tune to himself as he was contentedly figuring out the easiest way he would raise ten pounds to replenish the parochial housekeeping kitty.

Unemployment and Emigration

The Great Northern Railway (GNR), which ran from Foyle Road to Dublin, closed in 1964 with the loss of many jobs for men who, as well as their fathers and grandfathers, had spent lifetimes working in all the stations and workshops in every town along its route. My wife's grandfather, and other men who once lived in Mitchelburne Terrace on Foyle Road, worked there along with a few others including the Sweeney brothers, Johnny, Danny and George, who lived at the bottom of Bishop Street. A quiz question going about in those days was: What bar in Derry has no toilet? Answer: the one owned by Christian Johnston in the GNR station, because a person had to leave the bar and go along the platform to use the station toilet.

When the BSR factories in Bligh's Lane and Drumahoe, and the trainee factory in Pennyburn Pass, all closed in 1967, it caused great hardship and stress for hundreds of families in the town. At one time,

Five Walker's Square men in Arrington, England, in 1957 about to cook their dinners. Includes: Joe McQuaid, Tommy O'Neil, Unknown, Charlie 'Chang' McQuaid and Willie Organ. (Courtesy Paddy O'Neil)

the factories employed over two thousand people, whose quality of life had improved because of the steady wages that went into their homes. Many of the young men packed their cases and went to England to work, taking their skills with them. Some married English girls and set up permanent homes there, but the majority, some of whom had their own wives and young children back home, eventually returned to the town to find work when the employment situation in Derry had improved. Other unfortunate young and middle-aged people never worked again and ended their days on the dole and invalidity benefits.

I had the pleasure, in later years, to work in the Arntz Belting Company factory in Pennyburn alongside Danny Doherty, who was one of those who had gone from the BSR to England, only to return to his native city to search for work of any description. The following amusing story related to me, which I have slightly enhanced, was one of the numerous he told during the many years I worked alongside him before he suddenly passed away in 2001.

Sunny Side Up

Danny Doherty lived in the Lone Moor Road and had been searching for a permanent job ever since the BSR factory (which had at one time employed over two thousand young men) closed down in 1967, leaving him redundant at the age of twenty. He was now thirty-one and had toiled in England and in various temporary jobs in Derry's ailing construction industry, when he got work as a labourer at the building of the Lecky Road flyover in 1972. Around that time, adult education courses were becoming popular for those who wished to learn the subjects they neglected to take any interest in at school, when it was common practice for most Derry children to leave the classroom behind and find work at the age of fourteen. The more popular courses were English and maths, which were the basic qualifications required for a person to have any hopes of getting permanent employment in a local government office or the established businesses and factories.

Danny, wishing to take advantage of the chance to further himself in education, thus giving him hopes for better prospects in the employment field and get out of the rut, applied for a weekly evening course in English literature at the Strand Technical College. The classes were small, consisting of about eight young people who had the same intentions as Danny, with most of them barely able to write a few sentences, and with very poor grammar. Near the end of the course, the pupils were asked to write an essay at home and present it at the next evening class, where each would read their own piece to the tutor and the other students for assessment. The essay was to describe how each person saw the sunrises in their own localities, what it meant to them, and how it made them feel as they watched the dawning of a new day.

Danny worked at his piece in the quietness of his bedroom for three evenings after working all day hauling steel rods and barrowing concrete mixes at the construction of the new flyover and, as one can imagine, watching sunrises didn't loom too large in his head, because they only meant that he had to rise from the comfort of his cosy bed to begin another hard day's labouring on the Lecky Road.

At evening class that week, Danny was the first to read his essay about how the sun slowly rose from beneath the deep purple horizon like a golden ball of fire to caress the cold earth and rouse it from its soft, silent nocturnal slumber. He went on to describe his feelings as he marvelled at the miracle that took place each morning and had been occurring every morning since time began on earth. He was pleased with the applauded response given by his classmates and proud as punch when the teacher praised his homework.

Each of the others read their essays, some better and some very poor from the students who didn't put too much effort or thought into them. One female student in her late twenties, who lived near the border at Killea, caused amusement with part of her essay that read: *The sun comes up like a fried egg every morning over Killea and I can feel an excited hunger gnawing at the insides of my stomach as I also observe the two fir trees that stand at the bottom of our garden, framing it like two pork sausages, and the little wisps of cloud in the sky above reminding me of grilled slices of crispy bacon.* Broad smiles were on most of the faces in the classroom, with one or two of them holding in giggles as the teacher clapped her hands a few times as she commented, 'Everyone else gets the sun to rise over their part of the world, but the Killea people get something more special when a fried egg comes over the horizon at dawn.'

That English course was to set Danny on the road to further education and he was rewarded by securing employment for the rest of his working life in one of the local factories. He didn't become a professor or an academic, but he appreciated what learning he received and often I heard him say that without those English lessons he wouldn't have been able to read the horses in the papers or write out his bookie slips that won him quite a few rises. Also, he remarked, 'The Killea people only have a fried egg on sunny mornings, but for me, every day is sunny side up.'

The Changing 1960s

The 1960s saw great changes sweeping across Europe, Britain, Ireland and America, where, in 1963, the assassination of President John F Kennedy in Dallas, Texas, stunned and saddened the people of Ireland and the western world.

A L&LSR train passing St Patrick's Church, Pennyburn, on its way to Buncrana in 1949. (Courtesy Central Library, Derry)

The L&LSR yard at the foot of Buncrana Road in 1955.
(Courtesy Central Library, Derry)

Standards of living slightly improved for many families in Derry, especially for children and teenagers, whose education opportunities increased under the guidance of the excellent, highly skilled teachers in the local schools. Unfortunately, along with the changes came the beginning of the demise of the local shirt-making industry, which had been a traditional source of income for over 6,000 people at one time in Derry. The BSR factory was paying off hundreds of young men, and the railway systems were gradually being dismantled, with the closures of the GNR and the Strabane-Omagh links. Derry and its people also suffered a colossal body blow, delivered by the Stormont Government in 1965 (and aided by faceless members of Derry Corporation) when they hatched a scheme to rob the town of a much needed and valuable university and decided to build it in Coleraine in 1972.

Known retrospectively as the 'Swinging Sixties', the decade saw the introduction of the so-called permissive society, with the emergence of the 'Flower Power' message that manifested itself in everything from psychedelic fabrics to experimenting with hallucinogenic drugs and peaceful revolution by the 'Hippy Movement'. It reached its peak in the summer of 1967 in San Francisco, California.

The whole music scene, too, was changing, and teenagers were listening to the latest pop music nightly on Radio Luxemburg and Alan Freeman's *Pick of the Pops* on the BBC on Sunday evenings. Tony Blackburn and John Peel hosted two popular music programmes from pirate radio ships called Radio Caroline and Radio London, operating offshore, which the government closed down because of a risk to shipping. One of the more popular and lasting singer-songwriters from that era was Bob Dylan, whose new-age songs were about freedom and peace, and which finally swept the old, dreary music-hall singers off the entertainment stages. Simon and Garfunkel's *Bridge Over Troubled Waters* album was being played in many homes, and their songs are still played today.

Along came the Beatles and the Rolling Stones, who caused our older parents and strait-laced elders to frown and tut-tut at their long hairstyles that became fashionable with the youth. Many of the school principals laid down rules banning the longhaired fashion among boys from their classrooms. Three of my own boys who attended St Columb's College in the 1970s, and whose hair had just needed trimmed, were warned along with others to keep their hairstyles short and tidy or else they would be suspended from school until they did so.

On television, Cathy McGowan presented ITV's *Ready Steady Go*, and *Top of the Pops* was watched on the BBC. In the cinemas, Clint Eastwood starred in *A Fist Full of Dollars*; Sean Connery played the immortal British secret agent, *James Bond*. Dustin Hoffman acted in *The Graduate* and *Midnight Cowboy* with Jon Voight. *Butch Cassidy and the Sundance Kid* and *Doctor Zhivago* were also big attractions in Derry's cinemas.

We got our first TV, a reconditioned second-hand set, from a small electrical goods shop at the bottom of Creggan Road in 1965, and my children sat patiently waiting every evening to watch their favourite programmes, *The Flowerpot Men, Camberwick Green, Sooty and Sweep, Trumpton* and *The Magic Roundabout*. One night weekly, everyone settled down to watch the exciting *Doctor Who*, starring William Hartnell who was replaced by Patrick Troughton in 1966. In those days, when somebody called to visit, or came into the house to leave a message, or to have a short conversation, the TV's volume was turned down or the set switched off as a matter of courtesy and good manners. Habits and good manners have changed drastically over the years since then; now a person coming into the house sits down and silently watches until the programme, which is usually a soap opera, ends before they are acknowledged or recognised.

Three of the more popular toys introduced in the 1960s were: the Barbie fashion doll for girls; the Spacehopper, a large, inflated rubber balloon for sitting on with two handles; and the Action Man with his weapons of war, some of which had a recorded voice device inside that was activated when a string on the back was pulled. Nearly every boy in Derry had at least one Action Man. My own boys had six, along with their tanks and jeeps and weapons, and battles took place on top of the sideboard and under the settee and up on the kitchen table and all through the house and into the backyard every day, and if the soldiers had been real, the whole house would have tumbled down around us all.

We had one little girl, Carol, who had a Barbie Doll that kept her quiet and amused as she dressed and undressed it and combed its hair and talked to it as if it was a real live fashion model. When the Action Man battles were raging, Barbie, who had the experience of being a casualty before, had to be put safely away to avoid being battered and run over by a jeep. When the boys were sleeping, their Action Men were snugly tucked in beside them and their guns and vehicles stored safely under the beds until the next day's war was declared.

That particular favourite toy, along with the popular USA Marine soldiers' outfit, became very unpopular worldwide when the horrific scenes of maimed Vietnamese children and the destruction of their homes by American forces were exposed on television throughout the world.

Before it became unpopular, one of my boys got an imitation American Marine's uniform, complete with plastic helmet and rifle, from Santa Claus one year. After having my dinner one evening, I sat on the settee, watching the news on TV, and put on the helmet and began to tap my head with a metal toy handgun as I thought to myself, *I wonder if this helmet would protect a person if they were hit over the head with a weapon, or would it be painful?*

My wife was in the scullery, washing the dishes, and the younger children were playing about while the oldest sons, Patrick and Billy, did their homework at the table, and nobody paid any heed to me. In my silliness, I convinced myself that the headgear would save me if my oldest son, Patrick, who was about eight years old, hit me on the head with the toy gun. I told him to stand on the settee behind me and whack me, which he willingly did with great enthusiasm. I thought my head was split open with the force of the blow and let out a yell of pain as he jumped off the settee and ran, frightened, to the street.

I was sitting nursing a huge bump on the top of my skull when he peeped round the door to see if I was still alive and angry, and I called him over to me and asked him why he hit me so hard – a stupid question, I thought after I asked it. His answer was quite mature when he said, 'Da, what would you do if someone who gave you the odd slap on the backside and the odd clip along the ear for nothing, gave you an opportunity to hit them over the head?'

I burst out laughing and didn't answer as my wife called in from the scullery, 'You deserve that. And I hope it knocked those stupid notions out of your head.'

With the coming of the TV era, flashy new plastic toys and indoor games were easier to get, and with more traffic on the roads, it was becoming too dangerous for children to play on the streets anymore. The games they had played for generations were gradually fading out and fewer children swung round lampposts or played football in the middle of the road. Games of hopscotch on chalked-out squares where girls hopped about after a shoe-polish tin on the footpath – or tig, when one person had to run after a group of others to touch one of them to put the person out of the game – were too old-fashioned and boring compared to hula hoops, roller skates or watching the television. Skipping with ropes was usually a game played by girls, sometimes by one girl alone, or by two holding a long rope at either end and swinging it as other girls and one or two boys jumped over it in rhythm as they all sang rhymes together. The first lines of a favourite one being: *On the mountain stands a lady, who she is I do not know, she has lots of gold and silver, all she wants is Michael O'* – if that happened to be the name of one of the boys.

Little boys and girls played on the footpath at making a house and imitating a real family living in one of them. During a good summer day, the streets were filled with children playing at all sorts of games and running into their houses now and then to get a piece of bread to

Three McGill brothers from Nailor's Row along with Tommy O'Neil and some adults and children from Walker's Square on a day's outing in the early 1960s. (Courtesy Paddy O'Neil)

Whitewashing a house in preparation for St Columba's Day in Walker's Square in 1955. Includes: P Gillen, Jock Ramsey, Cody Maguire and S Ramsey. (Courtesy Paddy O'Neil)

eat or a drink of water. Unnoticed during that '60s decade was the gradual phasing out of old customs and mannerisms in Derry and the slow introduction of modern trends that crept into every fabric of society with each passing year.

Before the end of the 1960s, Russia and America sent men into space to orbit the earth and, by the end of the decade, men were walking on the surface of the moon.

Sporting World

In boxing, Englishman Henry Cooper, the holder of the British and Empire heavyweight titles, fought the world champion, Cassius Clay (later to be called Muhammad Ali) in England. Although Cooper lost the fight, he was one of the few to put Cassius on the floor with his famous left hook to the jaw. In case anyone has forgotten, England won

Foyle Harps supporters showing off the cup in the 1960s. Front: Willie McMonagle and Ronnie Ballard. Middle L to R: Painty Radcliffe, Wally Ferry, Cripper Meenan and Nya McFadden. Back L to R: Quigley, Jackie Power, Pa Meenan, Joe McKeever and Davy Porter. (Courtesy Masie McKinney)

Harps Supporters in the 1960s. L to R: Tom McGowan, P McSwine, J Radcliffe, S Brandon, D Kerr, H McLaughlin, G Crossan, T Cooley, J McNulty and T McGowan. (Courtesy Terry Francis)

The BSR Motors' Team in 1960, includes at back L to R: H Wade, P McCallion, Unknown, Pascal McCallion, Unknown, C O'Donnell, P Norris, J Moran, C Walker, E McDaid, Maxi McLaughlin, T McCallion, T Gibson, J Millar and J Clifford. At front L to R: P O'Neill, J Anderson, P McIntyre, W Elliot, S Rodgers, J McKeever, D Stevenson, M Doherty, T Anderson, G Gallagher and N Breslin. (Courtesy Dan O'Donnell)

Derry City FC, Irish League Champions in 1965. Back L to R: Matt Doherty, Billy Cathcart, Frank Connor, Dougie Wood, Eunan Blake and Ron Wood. Front L to R: Fay Coyle, Jimbo Crossan, Jimmy McGeogh, Joey Wilson and Roy Seddon.

Members of Pennyburn Youth Club jogging to keep fit in 1978. (Courtesy W English)

Oxford FC members and guests at a celebration function in 1974.
(Courtesy Noel Crampsey)

the World Cup in 1966 by beating Germany by four goals to two in Wembley Stadium. We in Derry had more important events to celebrate over the two previous years, when our local team won the Irish cup in 1964 by beating Glentoran 2–1 at Windsor Park, and the following year, in April 1965, won the Irish league for the first time when they beat Ards by five goals to one in the Brandywell. Fay Coyle, who played for Derry City between the years 1963 and 1966, was a valuable inspiration to the rest of the players in those two successful seasons. Over the three years he played with Derry, he scored seventy-seven goals.

Australia Bound and 'Reds'

Even with the times changing elsewhere for the better, housing conditions in Derry were still atrocious. The few new houses being constructed were allocated to those families from the streets being demolished in the redevelopment programme that was progressing at a very slow pace. Newly married couples were still finding great difficulty acquiring decent living accommodation and many were forced to emigrate. A government-controlled emigration scheme was introduced in the 1960s in an attempt to relieve the poor employment situation. By paying a large portion of the travelling costs, assistance was given to families to settle in Australia and to find jobs and homes. The Dohertys, who lived in Bishop Street in 1967, were one such family who took the plunge: the elderly parents, their married sons, Brian and Liam, and daughters, Sheila Hume, Rosemary Nash, Bridie Somers and Celine all departed. Among others who emigrated were members of the Connolly family from the Brandywell, one of whom, David, organised and still heads a successful and valuable Derry Emigrant Association with the purpose of helping Derry emigrants to keep in touch with each other and with their families back home.

When lack of housing became so bad in 1966, some young educated men, including Eamonn McCann, Fionbarra O'Dochartaigh and Eamon Melaugh, set up a housing action association. The purpose of the action group was to highlight the problem and agitate for the alleviation of the ever-lengthening homeless families' list. After a period

Part of St Columb's Wells at the bottom of Howard Street during redevelopment in 1972. (Courtesy Terry Francis)

Willie Cullen wondering what the future holds for him as his wife and one of their children happily play games in their one-room flat in Orchard Street in 1955.

A Derry Corporation cleaner keeping the neighbourhood spick
and span at the top of Wapping Lane in the 1960s.

of protests and letter writing, which was ignored by Derry
Corporation, the association members dragged a caravan, that was used
by the Corporation to house a large homeless family, into the middle
of Ann Street, an action that was condemned by the then moderate
Nationalist Party and its large following of supporters. They branded
the action-group members 'Reds' and followers of the Communist
Party which led to the members being disdained by the Churches and
Irish and British political and governing establishments.

The Ghost of Morgan's Rag Store

The rag store was where people went to sell their old clothes, including bedclothes that were patched and re-patched and worn out, until finally they went into the ragbag. Men and boys gathered pieces of scrap lead, copper and iron from old buildings to sell to the scrapyards, which was another way to get a few shillings for household needs or some pocket money.

James Morgan's rag store in the Lecky Road was where most people sold small pieces of lead and copper piping along with their old worn-out clothing. Every week or so when I was a teenager, my pals and I used to bring some rags that we had gathered from relations – as well as small amounts of scrap lead and copper – to sell in the rag store.

A few men, and one or two women, were employed to do various tasks in the store, such as weighing the customers' bags of rags and scrap metals, or sorting the woollens from other less valuable cotton and linen materials. Jimbo McCallion was one of those employed to cut the rags into strips before baling them for transportation.

One late autumn evening, he and two other young lads, Dickie and Tommy, were working overtime cutting up the clothes for baling in the top floor of the stores, which was said to be haunted by the ghost of an old man who lived there before the building became a rag store. The ghost could be heard making noises and shuffling about at times by the more superstitious workers. As they cut and chatted, the conversation turned to spooky happenings and the resident ghost.

The three men were feeling those little spine shivers and goose pimples on their skins when suddenly Dickie made a dash for the stairs with Jim and Tommy clattering hot on his heels until they reached the front door. Jimbo and Tommy were shaking and out of breath with fright as they tightly held Dickie by the arms and asked him repeatedly, 'What did you see, did you see the ghost?'

Dickie replied, 'Did youse not see it?'

'See what? Was it yer man, the ghost?' they asked.

'Naw,' said Dickie, 'did youse not see the size of the big bee that flew in the window?'

The fear was replaced by huge sighs of relief and the two now relaxed and happy men buckled up with laughter as they shook Dickie back to his senses. They made their way up the stairs again to finish the evening's work as they teased Dickie for being such a scaredy cat and afraid of a big harmless bee. When they were at the top of the stairs, they went silent and stopped in their tracks at the sounds of shuffling noises coming from the far corner of the top room.

Down the stairs they clattered again, but this time the three terrified men didn't stop until they were standing in the middle of the street, from which safe vantage point they looked up at the window of the top room. But nothing appeared. The only thing they saw was the big bee crawling out of the small opening at the top of the window and flying away towards the newly lighted street lamp and disappearing. Tommy closed up the rag store after they all had agreed that there was no more work being done, and off they went home.

Next morning, they related the whole frightening experience to the rest of their work companions and were overheard by the boss, James Morgan, who made his way up to the top room which Jimbo and his

Jim 'Jimbo' McCallion, storyteller and former resident of
Fahan Street, sticking it rightly in 2004.

Fahan Street in a dreary mood overlooking a smoky Bogside in the 1950s.

workmates had so hurriedly vacated the previous evening. As the workers attended to their various tasks, still discussing the eerie topic about the haunting, James came down the stairs, placed a cardboard shoe box in the middle of the floor and invited Jimbo to open it. Everyone gathered round to watch the lid being lifted off and Jimbo jumping back in horror when the contents were revealed. Three huge dead rats lay inside where James had placed them after he removed them from the traps a few minutes earlier. 'These long-tailed boys are the culprits that were making all those ghostly shuffling and rattling sounds in the upstairs room, and there are a few more to be dealt with,' he announced to the circle of surprised, wide-eyed spectators.

Everybody went back to work, some of them feeling a little disappointed that the excitement and the spooky atmosphere were at an end, and thinking that somehow having a friendly ghost upstairs gave the old, dreary, musty-smelling place a piece of class. That evening, as Jimbo, Dickie and Tommy were outside after locking up the store, Dickie asked the other two to stop and listen. The three men stood silently still and the hairs rose on the backs of their necks when

95

they heard scratching and screeching sounds coming from the slightly open window of the upstairs storeroom. Jimbo turned to his two ashen-faced workmates and said in a nervous quivering voice, 'If those dead rats were making all them eerie sounds, as James Morgan claimed, then who or what is making those same eerie noises now?' With no answer forthcoming, they each departed for home with a shiver of fear, the mystery still unsolved.

Good Neighbours

Families in Mary Street and Cooke Terrace whom I fondly remember, and who were very kind to us when we were rearing our children, included: our next door neighbours, Jackie and Sadie Kane; Pat and Mary Gormley; Ken and Ellen Mackenzie, whose father was a policeman when her family lived in Greenwalk in the Creggan estate; Emma Barr and her husband George, who worked as a salesman for

Some children from the Mary Street and Millar Street areas in 1974, posing on a sunny Saturday morning. Back: Philip Cunningham, Paul McGrory and Noel McGeehan. Middle: Mary McGrory, Brian Sweeney, Caroline McGrory and Carol Cunningham. Front: Kevin Carney, Joe Cunningham, Martin Tierney and Jim Sweeney.

Boys from St Columba's Long Tower Primary School on their Confirmation day in 1969. Included are priests Rev Fr J Carlin and Rev Fr Mulvey. Teachers, Mr S Kelly, Mr Harkin, Mr B Sharkey, Mr Doherty, Mrs O'Connor and Miss C Radcliffe. Pupils, Dermott Francis, D Roddy, D Boyle, N Smith, J McCloskey, L McDaid, T Irvine, J McLaughlin, D Doherty, M Browne, Gary Martin, Paul Radcliffe, J McGilloway, P White, A Flood, T McBride, H Crossan, J Curran, J Muldoon, A Corry, A Gormley and S McDaid. (Courtesy Mrs Teresa Roddy)

Residents from the Lecky Road and Lower Hogg's Folly pose for the camera beside the entrance to the CBS Brow of the Hill School in the late 1940s.

The CBS Brow of the Hill Confirmation class of 1946. At back L to R: A Moore, J Doherty; G Collins, L McGowan, Unknown and B Callan. Fifth Row: B Doherty; D Carroll, T Daly, M McDaid, Unknown, B McGowan and standing, Brother McNamara. Fourth row: D Keegan, R Browne, C Fox, F Curran, P Meenan, and G McCafferty. Third row: J Campbell, S Cowley; B Moran, J Lamberton, L Carlin and S Deane. Second row: D Sharkey, R Harkin, J Mallett, A Forsythe, D Loughrey, B McCafferty and J Campbell. Front row on ground: L Deane, E Doherty, K McCaul, B Coulter and J Murphy. (Courtesy Freddy Cunningham).

99

A large group of Brandywell residents proudly displaying their colourful flags and bunting on St Columba's Day in the early 1950s. (Courtesy Willie Cooley)

Jacob's Biscuit Company; Angela and her husband Jimmy Carney, who was an assistant in Austins Department Store in the Diamond that was owned by his cousin Larry Hasson; the McGrory Family, whose father Pat died when the six children were still at school. In Miller Street: Danny and Gretta Sweeney; Eddie and Agnes Tierney; John and Teresa McGeehan and seven sons; and the McPhillips, Jimmy and Rita, who had five sons and two daughters.

The Stipends

The Stipends fund was a special annual church collection of cash donations, diligently collected by a loyal band of committee members at every parishioner's front door throughout the Catholic Derry Diocese since the 1920s until it was replaced by the gradual introduction of the weekly church collections in the late 1950s.

The names of every head of each household were written into a ledger with the amounts of money written beside them. In those days, the majority of people weren't too well off and the usual donation was from

Howard Street upper in the 1960s before redevelopment.
(Courtesy John Bryson's *Streets of Derry*)

101

The Tower Bar in Long Tower Street in the more settled era of the 1950s.
(Courtesy John Bryson's *Streets of Derry*)

threepence to two shillings, with the amounts increasing to about five pounds the higher up the social ladder they went. On a certain Sunday of the year at all the Masses, the names, addresses and the amount each one had subscribed were read from the altar, one at a time, and the silence was only punctuated now and then as a red-faced, embarrassed person or family member coughed or shuffled their feet on hearing their name, along with their small or, worse still, *no* donation, being broadcast to every ear in the tightly packed, attentive congregation, many of whom were squirming and mortified as the house numbers in their street were getting closer and closer to themselves.

The half-crown and five-shilling donors sat in the middle of the church, whereas the balconies and rear were packed to the doors with the threepenny and sixpenny people. In the front seats sat the better off, along with the even richer people, among whom were the odd pretenders (usually women who wore fur coats but hadn't the nails to scratch themselves with), who always managed to get one pound written against their names just to get noticed. When their names were announced, they would put their chin up and look down their nose at those around them to savour their annual three seconds of glory. They were regarded as the 'fur coat and no knickers brigade', and nearly every street in Derry had one; they wouldn't let a child darken their doorstep, but never did harm to anyone.

The reading of the Stipends was a very uncomfortable experience to sit through for the vast majority of people in those days of scarcity and want. The practice mercifully petered out in the late 1950s when the weekly church collections were introduced and people's incomes improved slightly.

An equally unchristian practice was when the priest in charge read a person's name from the altar and denounced their unholy actions of marrying a person of a different religious persuasion from the Roman Catholic faith. The person was unable to receive the Holy Eucharist in the church and their family suffered the shame of being stared at and shunned by the rest of the parishioners. The practice of 'reading people off the altar' ended in the early 1950s and church-goers of every religious faith in Ireland were relieved, especially the couples who had entered into mixed marriages.

For many years, the Church hierarchy 'encouraged' pregnant women to receive a special blessing by a priest, usually in the sacristy or in the parochial house, shortly before her baby was born. (I remember accompanying my wife to be blessed in the Long Tower parochial house in Abercorn Road and waiting outside the door for her.) A few weeks after the baby was born, the child's mother had to go again to a priest and take part in a brief ceremony that was called 'Churching'. It was a ritual in which the mother was received back into the Church's favour again because she had conceived and given birth to a baby that had been in original sin. That practice for women quietly faded away by the end of 1960.

The Legion of Mary

The Legion of Mary is a worldwide organisation attached to the Catholic Church that had a large membership in Ireland in the 1950s and '60s. Its aim was to spread devotion to the Virgin Mary by visiting homes and asking people to become members, or else to say a special prayer, the *Magnificat*, to Mary every day. Every church in Ireland had a group of members, known as a presidium, which met weekly to pray together and to plan house and hospital visits by its members. I joined the Long Tower presidium in 1965, and for a while visited old and lonely people in their homes and sometimes visited sick people in hospital. The four or five visits, one night per week, only took a couple of hours of my time and I felt it a very rewarding experience. Jimmy Browne was a Legion member, as well as being a member of another voluntary and charitable organisation, the St Vincent de Paul Society, which collected money and second-hand items of furniture and clothes that were then distributed to the poor and needy people in the town.

Jimmy's charitable work included writing short, informative letters and snippets of harmless local gossip to Derry emigrants in every country in the world who had been away for a long time and who found it difficult to visit their relatives back home very often because of the expense involved. I gave up visiting homes and hospitals and went instead, along with Tommy McCay from Nailor's Row, to help Jimmy in his office – given rent-free to the Society – beside the minor hall in St Columb's Hall.

The caretaker of St Columb's was Jim Larmour, who lived with his wife and daughter in the building. As a matter of interest, Jim was the son of Johnny Larmour, who had a small second-hand shop in Nailor's Row, where he sold everything from a needle to an anchor in the 1950s. Through time, with the assistance of two teenage girls, Ann Martin and Ann Gallagher, who had been members of one of the local youth associations, we put a small booklet together called the *DEB*, the Derry Emigration Bureau, the name under which the office operated.

The *DEB* was published every month and contained short pieces of local information and extracts from some of the emigrants' letters that we received nearly every day. The booklet was posted to the emigrants and also sold for a few pence to Derry people who wanted to send copies to their own relatives in England, America and other countries. The Emigration Bureau was very successful in tracing families' relatives, especially those who had gone to England and hadn't made contact with home for a number of years. We had contacts with the Irish societies and Salvation Army in England who were extremely helpful and experienced in tracing many destitute Irish men and women in those years of high emigration from Ireland.

Scouts and Clubs

I gave up membership of the Legion and helped to form a committee to run the 7th Derry CBSI, Catholic Boys Scouts of Ireland, a scouting unit for boys living in the parish. The scouting unit leader, Paddy Roddy (from Lisfannon Park), was assisted by his brother, John, and

Some 7th Derry scouts and cubs in 1972. Includes: Back L to R: D Nelis, J Hutcheon, P Cunningham, Unknown and R McPhillips. Middle L to R: G Cunningham, P Cunningham, K Carney, N McGeehan, C McMonagle and Unknown. Front L to R: D Curran, J Cunningham and Unknown.

Brian Heatley. Billy Nelis and Reggie O'Connell organised and trained the cubs' pack of over thirty boys with the assistance of Tony O'Donnell and myself. Tony was also the chairman and treasurer of the unit committee, which included Maureen Owens and her sister Breedge O'Connell, Mary Desmond, and myself as the secretary. Billy, Reggie and I had sons in the scouts and cubs, along with boys from the Bogside and Bishop Street areas, and on Saturdays during the dry summer weather, we took the cubs out to Moore's Quay beside the Foyle along the old, disused GNR lines. Billy and I got boxes of nicky cake biscuits and packets of soup free of charge from the wholesale stores of O'Neill and McHenry at the end of Craigavon Bridge. Everything, along with two large urns in which to make the soup and tea, was carried to our venue, where fires were lit for cooking and canopies of branches were erected for shelter in case it rained.

As a rule, cubs were not allowed to go camping under canvas and when they went to stay overnight from home for a day or two, they

Scouts from St Mary's and Long Tower CBSI units in 1973. Back L to R:
J McDowell, P Boyle, M Gillespie, T Lynch, R Irwin, J Roddy, P McDowell,
J Hutcheon, M Meehan, C O'Doherty and A Gillen. Front: J Loughrey,
M Tinney, E McManus, G Green, M Power, P Cunningham and D
McLaughlin. (Courtesy John McDowell)

were put up in a parish hall or a youth club. The scouts were more advanced, and camped for a week in the unit's own tents every year in Ards in County Donegal with other units from Creggan, Waterside, Shantallow and Rosemount. The whole event and scouting activities were organised by the regional commander, Reggie Ryan, who was responsible for bringing the CBSI to Derry and setting up the 1st Derry Unit in the Creggan estate. Within a year of the 7th Derry being formed, the waiting list of boys got so long that we formed the 10th Derry Long Tower that had Bobby McGilloway as its unit leader, assisted by John Roddy.

The boys who lived in the streets between Bishop Street and Foyle Road, which included Sloan's Terrace, Orchard Row, McLaughlin's Close, Carrigan's Lane, Miller Street, Mary Street and Ferguson's Lane, had no facilities to play football or any of the other outdoor sports. Many of them joined a boxing club in a vacant house in Alma Place,

Pat Strain presenting the Tony Strain trophy to Joe Starrett from St Eugene's Boxing Club as Patsy Heavern, George McCann and Paddy Canning look on in the 1970s. (Courtesy J Starrett)

where my boys and their pals from the surrounding streets went four nights weekly to train. John Donnelly ran the club. His brothers, Len and Tommy, were also very much involved in boxing. Len was a professional during the reign of Billy 'Spider' Kelly, and Tommy coached and managed Charlie Nash who won the British and European lightweight crowns and fought for the world title.

When John Donnelly thought some of the boys were able and experienced enough to box strangers from other camps, he included them in a team to enter competitions. I remember one such contest, when the team of boys and club members travelled to some small village to box, and when they got there, the other team didn't show up. To avoid disappointing the patrons who had come to watch the fights, John made two teams from the boys in his own club and they competed against each other. Every boy who boxed that evening was presented with a medal or trophy, and two of my own boys came home with medals and big smiles. When Alma Place was demolished for redevelopment, John set up his boxing club in the Long Tower's newly acquired multi-sports premises in the Brandywell Showgrounds, where its membership dwindled and ceased because of the greater interest in

Harps supporters building the club hall in the Brandywell in the late 1940s.
Back: G McDermott, V Callaghan, D McCann, J McGeady, T Callaghan and
L McGuinness. Front: G Gallagher, Olive McDonnell and L Carlin.
(Courtesy Terry Francis)

108

soccer by the younger boys living in and around that district. Eugene O'Kane and Tommy McCann revived the boxing club again a few years later under the name of Oak Leaf, and its membership and success grew as a result of their hard work and dedication.

Markie Toland and his son ran the Long Tower Boys' Club in a large wooden hut he erected on disused GNR railway property at Foyle Road, where they played all sorts of indoor games. In the summer weather, he organised trips to Gartan, in Donegal, where they canoed and fished and stayed in a house beside the lake owned by the Long Tower Church. The club hut was maliciously burned down, however, and was never replaced, and with that valuable amenity for youth in the area gone, it meant that a few boys got up to all sorts of harmless mischief that annoyed some of their neighbours.

Harmless Mischief

Jimmy 'Smokey' Rodgers was a bachelor who lived in Ferguson's Lane with his relatives, the McGonagle family, some of who were popular singers in the local showband scene in the 1960s. Smokey, who always had a lean and dishevelled appearance, was of average height and often wore a black overcoat and cap. He worked on the docks and was fond of a wee drink now and then, and when he got one too many, people could hear him a mile away, because his voice got louder as he shouted or tried to sing on his way home from the pub. His speech became a deep, guttural, mumbled garble and no-one except his nephews could understand what he was trying to say.

One day as I was in the backyard of our house in Mary Street breaking sticks with an axe to light the fire, three of my young boys and three of their pals came running through the house from the front street. They ran past me out the back gate and down the mews lane behind our street and Ewing Street. I shouted after them to slow down, but they were in so great a rush that none of them paid any heed to me. Just then, I heard Smokey Rodgers shouting into my house from the street and I went to investigate what was bothering him. As I approached him at the front door, he ran, frightened, down the street, stopping now and then to look back and call me a hatchet man. I suddenly realised that I was still holding the axe and that was why he believed I was going to attack him. I questioned my sons later that day and chided them for annoying Smokey Rodgers. The next time I met him, I apologised for my thoughtlessness and my children's mischievous behaviour towards him.

The Bath Boat

I was at the top of a ladder, painting the front of the house, one warm, sunny Saturday evening, and as I worked away quite happily, I heard Jamsie O'Hagan, who lived in Foyle Road, calling me. He looked flustered as he came rushing up the street and stopped at the foot of my ladder. When I asked him what was wrong, he told me that he and his wife, Rosie, were looking out of their top bedroom window that overlooked the Foyle and saw my son, Gregory, crossing the river in an old white bath. We both ran down to Foyle Road and into the disused railway yard beside the river to see if Gregory was about and met Jamsie's son, Eddie, who was Gregory's pal. He told us that an old bath had been dumped at the edge of the river and he had taken a plug from his ma's house and stuck it in the plughole. Then they launched the bath into the river, where Gregory climbed into it and stood with one foot on the plug to keep it in place. With the aid of a flat piece of wood for an oar, he had paddled across the Foyle to the other bank in the Waterside.

I looked across the river and saw the tiny figure of a boy standing at the far side, waving over at us. I also noticed a lot of people on Craigavon Bridge looking in our direction. They had been watching the whole scene and I began shouting to Gregory to come back over the bridge. I didn't know whether he heard me or not, but when he returned safely, he got a good telling off from his mother and me. But our scolding was like putting water on a duck's back, because all the boys played along the river at one time or another, and some were falling in, or coming home with their shoes and clothes muddied in those days when there were no other amenities or play areas provided for children in the district.

Postal Charity Mislaid
(An old Derry tale revived)

Dorothy Deeney, a spinster aged sixty-two and living on her meagre state pension, was finding it difficult to make ends meet, especially with Christmas being only five weeks away. She needed some new clothes for herself and some money to buy extra fuel and a few presents for her young nieces and nephews, as well as a few little gifts for her closest friends and neighbours on top of all that.

Frequent requests in her prayers to her favourite saints – Anthony, Martin, Joseph and Theresa – seemed to be going unanswered. Feeling unhappy that she would be regarded as ungrateful by everybody who had shown her kindness and love over the past year if she didn't buy them presents, an idea suddenly entered her head. Although she had long since stopped believing in Santa Claus, she believed that somewhere in the country, there must be a nice place where children's letters to Santa went, requesting toys and presents on Christmas morning.

'It's worth a try,' she thought as she wrote her letter, which read:

Dear Santa,

I'm in desperation, as I haven't enough money to make my Christmas happy. I need to buy some presents for a lot of good people and get some warm clothes for myself, but you see, I only get the old-age pension and didn't get enough money saved up this year, because I went on a week's holidays to Moville at the end of the summer with some new friends I met in our local community centre during the past year. If you could possibly send me fifty pounds, I would be so grateful and happy that other people and children would also benefit from the gesture of goodwill.

The letter was duly posted to Santa Claus, care of the General Post Office, Great James Street, where it went to the head supervisor, who examined all the letters that hadn't been properly addressed. As one might well imagine, Dorothy's wasn't the only letter addressed to Santa that ended up in the head supervisor's office. There were dozens of children's letters that were read and acknowledged by the Post Office, in keeping with the Christmas spirit so as not to disappoint all the children whose parents would be filling the stockings with the requested toys.

Dorothy's letter was pinned on the GPO notice board to be read by all the sorters and postmen. They felt sorry at the old lady's plight at Christmas time and decided to have a collection among themselves in an effort to raise the fifty pounds to make her happy in this special season of the year. However, the amount raised was only forty-three pounds – still a very charitable gesture from the sorting office – and it was specially delivered through Dorothy's letterbox on 20 December, giving her enough time to do her precious shopping and complete her seasonal errands.

Dorothy heard the rattle of the letterbox and collected her mail, which consisted of six Christmas cards from her friends and one from Santa Claus wishing her a very merry Christmas, and a few lines saying that he got her letter and was delighted to send her some money to buy some lovely gifts for her friends and relations.

On Christmas-eve morning in the sorting office, another letter from Dorothy to Santa was sitting on the head supervisor's desk; he opened it and it read:

Dear Santa,

Thank you for sending the money, but there was only forty-three pounds in it, because those thieving bastards working in the sorting office took seven pounds from it.

Happy Christmas,
Dorothy Deeney

Moral of the story: There's no pleasing some people!

The End of Old Derry

The chronic lack of proper housing and employment still plagued the town, where a slow redevelopment programme saw only families from the demolished streets being re-housed in the Foyle Hill and Creggan

The old and the new, both now gone. A group of children playing in Ann Street
as the Rossville Street high flats are being constructed in the 1960s.
(Courtesy John Doherty)

Residents of St Columb's Wells gathered around the blessed water pump on St Columba's Day in the 1940s. (Courtesy David Bigger collection)

Estates, the Woodlands near Muff in County Donegal, or in some far-off rural areas in the Waterside that were alien to them, such as Strathfoyle, Curryneirin and Gobnascale on the Strabane Old Road. Many of those desperate people were reluctant to be parted from their friends and neighbours, especially the older folks, some of whom hadn't travelled over the city boundary since they were children on their annual bus run to Buncrana. In the end, they were forced to go to those far-away places so they could have decent homes of their own along with their families. Many families living in overcrowded houses in the maze of streets between the Lecky Road, Rossville Street, William Street and the Lone Moor Road were eventually re-housed in their own areas. The building of the flyover caused the dispersal of families who lived in the tiny streets between Bishop Street and Hogg's Folly, which was also demolished.

During September 1968, a few attempts were made by concerned people who belonged to a variety of different shades of political groupings, to hold protest meetings in the town centre about the lack of civil rights in N Ireland. At the end of that month, an open-air meeting was held in Foyle Street but had to be abandoned because of the heavy presence of hostile RUC personnel. It was decided that day by the group to hold a protest march the following Saturday evening, on 5 October, to demand civil rights and liberties, and that everyone in Northern Ireland be allowed to vote in council, Stormont and Westminster elections. William Craig, the Minister for Home Affairs in the Stormont Government at the time, banned the march. However, the organisers went ahead and assembled with a few hundred determined men and women at the Waterside Railway Station and began their journey along Duke Street, intending to walk to the Guildhall Square.

When the marchers were beaten and water cannoned off Duke Street by the RUC that fateful day, it heralded the beginning of the end of old Derry, with its generations of close-knit, gentle-mannered people, many of whom had gone to the same schools and churches and had grown up together in the small, overcrowded streets below Derry's Walls; people who had endured many severe hardships and enjoyed even happier times when everybody knew everyone else's relatives and what they were having for their dinners, because nearly all the front

Residents of the Fountain area under a celebration arch in Wapping Lane in the 1960s. (Courtesy E McDowell)

Above: Vinny Coyle directing operations in Rossville Street in the 1970s. Right: Vinny Coyle, affectionately called 'Jim Figgerty' because of his resemblance to an actor in a 1960s television advertisement for Jacob's fig roll biscuits. Vinny was an imposing, larger than life character, greatly respected as a chief steward during the many 1960s and '70s civil rights marches. (Courtesy Eamon Melaugh's Cain Collection)

Far right: Paddy 'Bogside' Doherty looking good in his retirement years as he strolls through Derry's town centre in July 2004.

Right: Dominic 'Chalk in the Water' Gallagher in his retirement years.

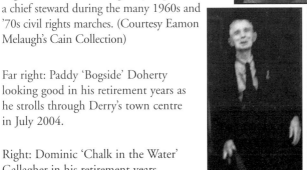

Lower Bishop Street religious arch in the 1930s. (Courtesy Paddy O'Neil)

doors were either open at all times or were on the latch to welcome one and all to enter and have a cup of tea and share the latest 'bars'. Those same people and their offspring were to suffer severe penalties lasting for many years for daring to ask the governing authorities in Ireland, England and the Six Counties to recognise and grant them their basic human rights as citizens of their own country of Ireland, and to be regarded as normal people.

Many volumes of tears and life's blood were to flow to the River Foyle over the succeeding years. I recall listening to older men and women when I was a young boy, saying that Derry's patron saint, Columba, had prophesied in the sixth century that the River Foyle would run red with blood before the end of the twentieth century. That was how the older generation in Derry would have simplified events they could not fathom or explain, when they believed that God had our lives laid out for us, and our fate should be willingly accepted without question. Not so with the present, more educated young population, most of whom demand truthful answers and honest treatment, and many of them, rightly or wrongly, wanting retribution and restitution for the misdeeds of the past and present by every authority that controls their futures.

The Royal Visit
By Philip Cunningham

Prince Charles came to Derry once, on a warm and sunny day,
To meet the Mayor and all his people, and to get a boul of tae.
He wore a big fur hat from a fox he himself had shot dead.
Why, it must have been a hundred degrees inside that royal head.
The Mayor and all the council walked him round to see the town.
They all crawled up our Shipquay Street before they all slid down.
Around the Derry Walls he walked and gawked down at the Bog,
And a wee boy yelled up at him, 'Git away home, ye dirty dog.'
Another one called up, 'Take that cat off your big fat crown.'
But Charlie just stood there grinning and didn't shout back down.
The sweat was running down his cheeks, the Mayor he then did say,
'Your Royal Highness, why wear that hat on such a nice warm day?'

'Well, when I was leaving home,' he said, 'my mum asked me to where?
When I told her Londonderry, she frowned and gave a stare.
*She scratched her head in wonderment and said, "Where the f***'s that?"*
And I always do what mummy says, so there's your answer, Pat.'

Displaced People

Near the end of 1969, shops and homes at the top of Bishop Street were destroyed when marauding extreme Unionist factions came out from the Fountain Street locality and firebombed them. Many properties, including the small shop where William Hippsley and his family lived, were left burning, and I remember seeing a line of B Specials blocking the road to prevent men from going to try and salvage their stricken families' belongings. The much used and loved establishment of Barr's Pawnshop was looted before it went up in flames that evening, and God only knows how many 'Da's suits' went up as well, leaving vacant spaces in many people's wardrobes and lives.

Many more families were displaced because of the civil unrest that continued for decades after. Homes in William Street behind the old Rossville Hall were damaged by fire when the hall was set alight, and the families had to be housed in caravans in the Brandywell Showgrounds and St Columb's Park in the Waterside. Denis and Gertie Crumlish and their seven young children, who lived below Shannon's old laundry facing the Devenney home, were the first to require emergency assistance. In the months to follow, a great number of Protestant families, worried about their own safety, moved from Rosemount and the greater Bogside areas to new homes in the Waterside, some of them from Mary Street and Ewing Street being my closest friends and neighbours.

I felt so fortunate and privileged to be living along with my wife and family of six children in Mary Street; another baby boy was destined to join us later. Rosita's parents had been living in Pennyburn since they were married in 1934, and some of her five brothers and two sisters were living there and in England. My three stepbrothers and two stepsisters and two cousins, all of whom lived with us in the back of the Walls,

Crossan's Pawnshop at the junction of Fox's Corner and Rossville Street, with Dinny Harley's fish and chip shop on the far right in the 1950s.

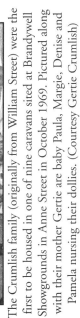

The Crumlish family (originally from William Street) were the first to be housed in one of nine caravans sited at Brandywell Showgrounds in Anne Street in October 1969. Pictured along with their mother Gertie are baby Paula, Margie, Denise and Pamela nursing their dollies. (Courtesy Gertie Crumlish)

were now married and settled. All my sisters were now married and housed: sister Margaret and Eddie Moore in the high flats in Rossville Street; Susie and Eamon McDowell in Foyle Hill Estate; Helen in America, and Mary and Ken Hannigan in Antrim. My brother and his wife, Freddie and Martha, were temporarily living in England. Uncle Freddie died in our Creggan home, and Danny, my youngest brother, and my Aunt Julia were still living in Creggan along with my parents ever since they had moved there with fourteen other souls all those years ago in 1950 from Friel's Terrace in the shadow of Derry's Walls.

The last few remaining inhabited houses, along with remnants of Nailor's Row, Friel's Terrace and Walker's Square, would become rubble by the end of 1972 as the pages of a new era of history were about to be written. Left standing alone on top of his pedestal would be our once-silent neighbour, the Rev George Walker, who would also soon be gone. His statue, like many of its kind, had its back to the Bogside and Creggan, ignoring the unfolding events behind him as he pointed towards the site down the River Foyle where the ship Mountjoy broke through the boom that had been placed across it, thus ending the siege of Derry in 1690, an important action in history that changed and moulded our lives (and those of our ancestors) to the present day. Some people still longingly look back on those days of old and are afraid to turn their faces forward along with the vast majority of citizens in the North who are longing for more agreeable and peaceful times.

The Rev George Walker's statue in the 1960s before its downfall from Derry's Walls.

Rossville Flats being demolished at the end of the 1980s.

Dedication, Toil and Music

Noel Henderson and his wife Ann, who had three children, lived in George and Emma Barr's house after they had moved to the Waterside. Noel's mother, Kathleen, visited him every week and I spoke to her often.

Kathleen Henderson, her husband Hugo and their five children were among the first to live in the Creggan estate in 1947 when they moved into Beechwood Crescent from a small upstairs flat in Laburnum Terrace. Their scant pieces of furniture from the flat were taken to their new home by pony and cart, which wasn't unusual then; many other families did likewise, because furniture removal vans weren't so common in those early years. Creggan Broadway was just being built and there were only a few houses on the one side of Inishowen Gardens.

The household of five children increased to twelve, the oldest being Pat and the youngest Brendan. After living happily there for fourteen years, Hugo, a piano tuner, died suddenly on board a bus that was taking himself and Kathleen on a pilgrimage to Knock Shrine. Life became a challenge for Kathleen, who had to struggle, working part time in some of the local small shops every evening from six o'clock until after midnight. She believed that education was a very important element for her family's future and made sure they understood by the example, encouragement and dedication that only strong-willed and loving mothers like her could give. Kathleen's determination and labours finally saw her family in secure careers and owning a successful piano and musical instrument business establishment in the city. Kathleen Henderson passed away peacefully on 8 August 2003, at the age of eighty-six.

As I spoke to Kathleen one day, she told me some fascinating stories of growing up in Derry from when she was born in 1917. She had actually recorded a brief but rich account of her life around 1992 and her son Noel passed a copy of it on to me. I wish to relate it here in her own words as it was written by her so as not to take away from its simplicity and beauty.

A Fire in the Wood
By Kathleen Henderson

Many years ago, in a two bed-roomed house in Derry, a little red-haired girl came into the world and it wasn't long until she started growing up. At the age of three, she went to school with her sister, Mary. I can well remember it was the 'Wee Nuns'; it just closed down recently in 1985. A few years after starting the Wee Nuns, I graduated up the chapel yard to St Columba's Girls' School.

I was in my heyday then. I used to look out of the window, and mostly every day I would have watched my father passing by in his railway uniform, and some days I would have seen my mother. It was great to see the people during the school hours, even if it was only through a window. I remember well one summer's evening after my uncle had his dinner, we took a walk down William Street. I remember wearing a green velvet frock covered with a white pinafore. I took off the pinafore and put it my uncle's pocket. Then I really felt dressed and I skipped along, hanging on to my uncle's arm with my long, red hair flying in the wind.

My uncle and I got a ride on a horse-drawn sidecar, and I loved the sound of the horse's hooves rattling on the cobblestones and trotting down to the quay when the driver had passengers to lift from the boat. I think it must have been the *Scotch Boat*, as there was a daily sailing there. We went down the steps at the quayside and got into the little ferryboat that took us across the river to the Waterside. Well, I thought I was going to America, and I was positively sure I was in America when I reached the other side. On our journey, we got some apples, and I remember asking my uncle if they were American apples. When I was told, 'No,' and asked why I thought they were, I replied, 'I can taste America off them.' My uncle laughed at this. We finished our evening by going into a bar and I remember sitting on a big high chair at the counter. No-one bothered in those days about children being in a bar. However, when we got back home, my father was late going to his work, as he had been looking for me, and it was important that he was at the railway station on time. My uncle got a good telling off for taking me away.

During the summer holidays, I used to go to Victoria Bridge in County Tyrone; it's a lovely country place, just a few hours away from Derry. I spent six weeks there every summer. The wood was opposite my auntie's house; it was called Paddy's Wood and I went down there every day; I knew every wee place around the wood. There were lovely willow trees and hazelnut trees. I often gathered nuts and also wild woodbine, which is a scented flower. It was so pleasant, with all kinds of birds singing, and rabbits and hares running about. I will forever remember the beauty of Paddy's Wood. At the bottom of the wood, there was the River Mourne. I used to cross to the other side on the stepping-stones at a shallow part of the river. When my father would come looking for me, he could easily identify me by the colour of my red hair; it stood out amid the green bushes and trees, and he used to say, 'There's a Fire in the Wood.' Those were great days, with no sweets, biscuits or money, just playing with the things that nature provided. I didn't need anything more to make me happy.

My father died at the age of forty-three when I was nine, and shortly after, my uncle died at the age of forty-five. I thought that it was a very young age for them both to die. When I was thirteen, I was allowed to go down to the railway station, because my brother was now working there. Behind the station were the tender boats that took people to

Kathleen Henderson playing the keyboards in the family music shop in 2003.

America, by travelling from Derry Quay to Moville, where they boarded a big ocean liner. I used to feel sad for the people who were emigrating then in 1929, because they were all crying and holding on to their loved ones.

I remember looking at them, and there was this one lady on the quay who asked me to hold a parcel and a big umbrella until she went to the toilet. I was still standing there, holding tight to my parcel and gazing about, but the lady didn't come back. There were about one hundred people there, between passengers and others, just watching the boat leave. My eyes searched everywhere for the lady. I was afraid to move; the lady just seemed to vanish into thin air. The next thing I was aware of was the noise of the boat when it started to move, and everyone was waving and crying. I suddenly saw the lady looking over the side of the boat, and I waved the bag and umbrella as high as I could. She recognised me, but there was nothing I could do. I left the quayside and took the parcel home; it contained three ladies' hats. However, my mother was very angry with me and told me I shouldn't have gone to 'those places'. I often wished that the lady had sent me a message through the paper so that I could have given back her hats and umbrella.

I did all the errands for my mother; she trusted me to get the right things, and so I ran here, there and everywhere after school. Before I went to school each morning, I would go to the bakery to get four stale loaves; mother thought they were just right for eating. We used to queue, where my Granny Graham always kept me a place, from 7.30 in the morning to get the bread.

After I left school, I went to the Londonderry Technical School and took up bookkeeping and commercial arithmetic. I also went to embroidery and hairdressing classes.

At the age of fifteen, I left education and started to work in Lipton's Grocery Shop in Bishop Street. My mother thought we were really well off, as it was the 1930s then and it was the 'Hungry Thirties'. I was sent from school to take a test, and the manager told me to start the next morning at 8.30. I didn't get much of a chance to think about it, I just had to get up and get to it. I worked hard and I loved it, and even had the privilege of getting a few sweets now and then.

I wore a white coat while I was working and got my long hair cut; I had started to grow up. My life had changed; I was a bit subdued then. Things started to improve at home; my elder sister and brother were now also working. I bought myself a Raleigh Sports Model bike; it was a nice wee bike and I paid up 2/6 every month for it. That was the only way you could have got a bike in those days. I really loved it and used to go to Buncrana in the evenings and to work on it in the mornings. Sometimes I would take off at 6.00am and go out the Letterkenny Road and just sit by the roadside to take in the lovely spring morning and hear the birds sing. Then I would go back, get my breakfast, go to Mass and then off to work. Those were great days.

A lady who lived in the Lone Moor Road gave me piano lessons; she charged 2/6 weekly for two days. When I started working, I saved £2 out of my wages every week and I bought a white piano at an auction and the man gave me a white chair into the bargain. I didn't know anything about pianos, as I was just fifteen. Well, I kept it for about two years and then I had saved up £7 and bought a better piano. I paid £5 for it and he took the white one in part exchange. I didn't know until about five years later that the old boy had done me in the deal. I met my husband, who was a piano tuner, and when he examined the piano, he found it to be a disaster. Soon after that, I got married and left the piano behind me. I didn't have to worry about it after that, as my husband provided the best pianos that could be got.

Thursday afternoons were half-day closing in the shops and I would go around on my bike to collect orders for Lipton's shop. I did a lot of business in Limewood Street, Beechwood Street, Stanley's Walk and

Hogg's Folly, and also the Ebrington Barracks in the Waterside – that's what it was known as then. I had a lot of sergeants and officers as customers there, billeted in the front and rear blocks, and they all gave me orders. I brought my orders in to Lipton's shop on Friday mornings and the message boys would put them up and deliver them that day. Then I used to go on the train up to the village of Sion Mills and collect orders from a man who had a small shop there. In Lipton's grocery store, we put sugar into 1lb packages. It was a great store, with no opposition, and it was the main shop in Bishop Street, near the Diamond. And strangely enough, the piano shop I work in now with my sons is just next door to where I first worked.

I worked in Lipton's shop each day to 6.00pm and it was very cold, with no heat at all; we were just told to work hard and keep warm. On Friday nights, we worked until 8.00pm, but on Saturday nights, the shop stayed open until 9.00pm, and most nights it was about 10.30pm or 11.00pm before you got finished. But I just loved that; after all, it was a place to go to and saved you from having to go any place else.

The busiest time was Christmas, with everyone doing their shopping. I remember it was 1.00am on Christmas Eve night when we got finished,

Ferryquay Street free of traffic in earlier days.

but I loved every minute of it. You walked home with all of your presents; then again, you had to go to work on Christmas day for a couple of hours also. This I really enjoyed, because you got new clothes for Christmas and it was great excitement putting on your very best. How I remember those lovely Christmas times; no wonder I feel sad when I look back.

During my life as a single girl, I started to go to the dances. The Corinthian Ballroom, the Memorial Hall, Ashfield Hall and the West End Hall were all popular dancehalls in Derry. Admission to most dances was only fourpence, but the bigger dances could cost about 2/6. At the Corinthian, you wore an evening dress. I remember one dance I went to in the Corinthian: it was my first dance and I fell down the stairs and knocked the heel off my shoe. I was so embarrassed I had to hide in a corner all night. I had quite a number of boyfriends in my day, which made me happy.

Then I used to go with friends after work to Buncrana on the train. The trip cost sixpence; it was known as a bathing ticket and the train was packed. Everyone was running down the Strand Road heading for the railway station. The train left at 7.30pm and went to Buncrana and returned at 10.30pm. There was great fun on the train, which was packed to the utmost; boys were hanging on the running board, and some were so bold that they climbed on top of the carriages. Everyone was so happy with just the fare down on the train and lucky enough to have a couple of pence to buy a penny bag of chips on the way home.

My good, free-and-easy days were soon to end. I met my husband at a party. Hugo played the piano-accordion and the song he was playing as I entered the room was *Love Walked Right In*, so he attributed that song to me. A couple of months later, he married me, and my lovely freedom disappeared. But sure I loved him, too, and said, 'I do.'

On 5 June 1939, I had a beautiful wedding in white wedding attire. I thought I was just lovely, at least my husband said so. We went to Belfast for a week on our honeymoon. The big day was soon over and I settled down in a wee village called Lifford in County Donegal. My husband worked as a clerk in the County Council Offices in Lifford, and after nearly ten months of marriage, I had my first child, a girl named Pat, but fate didn't let me stay long in my wee thatched cottage, as my brother got drowned while on a holiday with me. I was ill then and didn't like the surroundings any more.

While I lived in Lifford, I cycled up and down to Derry once a week. I loved going down the Letterkenny roadway; the roads were very bad, but the scenery was beautiful. I really got good value out of my bike and I went everywhere on it. I used to sign on the brue twice a week. I got fifteen shillings and I gave my mother ten and spent the balance going back on the train (the train cost 1/6). I got off at Strabane and cycled home to Lifford. My mother had no-one working and that was why I gave her the ten shillings to help her, but that just lasted ten months.

I went back to live in Derry when the war was still on. We had a flat in Laburnum Terrace, mind you it was only a one-room apartment and I now had three children: Kay was a new baby, only ten days old; Pat, who was two years old, and Jimmy, being the second, was one year when I went there and nearly six when we left. I used to take the three of them out in the pram; it was a great big pram that held the three of them. I took them down to their granny's in Elmwood Street. There I would wash their clothes, as I had no facility in Laburnum Terrace. I did my mother's washing as well; this took care of my days. And when it came 5.30pm, I packed the pram and got ready to go back home again. I spent all my nights and days with the children because my husband was working in Belfast, but of course he came home at the weekends.

I had another wee baby that I named Olive; she only lived a couple of days. She was born and died in the City and County Hospital. A year after that, I got Don. He was a handsome wee lad with blond, curly hair; I used to set him up on the table to fix his curls and I taught him to sing *The Homing Waltz* and several other songs when he was quite young. Two years later, Noel was born in the City and County Hospital at Christmas time. I was in the hospital over Christmas, and Santa came and gave Noel a wee pair of bootees. Well I think Noel must have brought in luck when he was six weeks old, because I was offered a house in Beechwood Crescent. I ran up Beechwood Avenue one night to where the house was. I left Jimmy in charge, and he was only five, and I remember him saying that he would count to a hundred until I got back. When I saw the house, I said to myself, 'My God, what a mansion!' I ran down Beechwood Avenue and down the Goat's Path with my heart full of pride and joy, knowing I had a house at last that I waited six years for.

I could hardly sleep that night with excitement, and the next day I started packing. I hadn't much to pack, and being on my own made it that much harder, but I was getting used to doing things on my own. I engaged our vegetable man to move my furniture. He had a donkey and a small cart and made a couple of runs up Beechwood Avenue to our new house. My son, Jimmy, was only five years old and he held on to the cart to give it his little support. After we got settled in our new house, it was lovely, and I told the children they couldn't go upstairs, as they hadn't seen stairs before and it might be dangerous. We were all very happy, but money was very scarce.

I only weighed between seven and eight stones, but I always had good health, thank God, for I hadn't much else. Both the children and I slept downstairs in the living-room for the first night, as I hadn't any beds upstairs as yet. I had a big settee, two cots and two prams, so we had plenty to sleep on, and we all huddled together, as it was so cold in that month of February. The weekend we moved into the house, Hugo, my husband, came home from Belfast. He met me in my mother's house in Elmwood Street. We put the children into the pram and went up the hill to our new home. Hugo was delighted and said it was the best house he had seen, in such a lovely area and with no houses in front of us. We were very fortunate to get that spot and were the first to arrive in the Creggan estate at that time. We had our ups and downs, and Jimmy used to gather sticks so we could have a good fire. It was great to see all of the children's lovely wee faces sitting around the fire and me telling them stories that they loved dearly. They loved the true stories about myself. I used to get library books and tell some good stories from them – there was no television in those days, only the wireless.

After I put the children to bed, I used to stay up to 5.00am, because I used to hire a washing machine costing 2/6 for an hour. I took it at night-time to get it that extra bit longer, and I really got my 2/6 worth. I washed and washed all night long and then hung out the washing on four lines. It was like the bleach green at Ardmore after a year in Beechwood.

One year after we moved in to our house, I got another baby son, Brian, and a little girl, Rose Marie, the year after. After I had Rose Marie, my husband decided it was time to come home from Belfast. Mind you, it was rough looking after all those children, just steps and stairs and very little money. I only got £3.10s to feed and clothe us all and I couldn't go to work, what with the children. Well then I got Carol and then Gerry, Philomena, and then the two youngest, Brendan and Deirdre. They were all beautiful children. I had one more child and he died. I worked late at night in a nearby shop at the top of Beechwood Avenue, got up early each morning, and I felt very upset about the new baby dying. Mind you, it was nearly 10lb weight. I know myself I didn't get any help, and if I had, I think it would have made a difference.

Hugo started piano tuning. He had previously done tuning when he was younger, but there was a time when no-one bothered to have their pianos tuned, money was so scarce. However, he put an advertisement in the paper for piano tuning and got two replies. I remember clearly, a man came to the door and asked if this was the house where the piano tuner lived. He wanted a length of piano wire and Hugo was able to give it to him. Another person came and asked if I had a shank to repair his hammer. So after a few tall orders like that, his business picked up and he started doing jobs for the schools and colleges, and soon things were looking up. Hugo would take Jimmy and Don along with him when he went to tune.

If they were in a church to fix an organ, Jimmy would get fed up and his daddy used to say, 'That fellow isn't coming with me again.' But Jimmy didn't mind, he was kind of glad. Don seemed to like going with his father, and he would have helped him by handing him the correct tools required. Hugo was pleased with him and used to get Don and Jimmy to wash his car and they would have earned a few shillings for that. Noel or Brian didn't go with their daddy to tune, because they were too young and got in the way.

Well, we got a phone; that was something! It was a luxury in those days to have one as well as the car, and having both was a move in the right direction.

After my family of twelve was complete, the worst was yet to come when my husband died. That was the biggest blow to my life and I

No Playstations or quad bikes to amuse the weans in those days. A junior body-building competition outside the Shantallow Community Centre in 1975. (Courtesy Dan O'Donnell)

didn't know where to start or what to do. You could say I had two families, a big one and a small one; the youngest children being from two to nine years, and the older ones from nine to eighteen years. Hugo died on the way to Knock Shrine in County Mayo in the month of May. We were travelling by bus and were only halfway there when he died on the roadside on the outskirts of Sligo. I will never forget that day and always remember him saying that it was a lovely day and quoted that there would be a change of weather on the way back to Derry. However, he never saw the change.

I remember crying on that bus and asking Hugo not to die and leave all the children for me to care for. The children were expecting us back around midnight. However, I arrived back before that, at about 8.30pm in a hearse, with Hugo in the coffin. I can still see my children's faces; they were frantic, to say the least. I attribute my success with my family to Hugo, as he obviously helped me along the way, and I will continue his good work when I am gone and watch over my own children and my grandchildren. My husband was a good provider. He was very intelligent and held good jobs at Harland and Wolfe and with an American firm called Mernett and Chapman.

All my children got good educations. It didn't cost one shilling to educate them. Jimmy got his exams; Don, Brian and Gerry went through St Columb's College; Noel went to the technical college and Brendan had success, too, with his education. The girls also did well: Pat did her secretarial exams; and Kay, Rose-Marie and Deirdre went to technical college; Philomena and Carol went to Thornhill.

Every one of my children is musical and can all play instruments. Pat and Carol are beautiful singers and indeed, all the rest of them can sing. Their father, Hugo, rest in peace, was very musical. He and his brother were in the Savanna band in their younger days. It is now that I am happy and proud of my twelve children and they are making it good on their own. They don't need their mammy any more, but they wouldn't agree with that.

I am forty-three years living in the same house that I bought recently for £6,000. Now that I am in my elderly years, I can work with my two sons, Brian and Brendan, in the piano shop, namely, Henderson's Music in Bishop Street. I do all the ordering of books and sheets for all different grades of music and I just love my work. When I'm at home, all I do is bake, and my specialities are scones and apple cakes. Apart from baking, I make my own jam in the fruit season, ginger wine during all the seasons and cook three times a day every day. I've started making hot lemon drinks morning and night for Brendan and myself; I think we'll probably turn into lemons soon enough. He's the only one left with me. God love him, he's great. Mind you, all my wains are great. My life is well worth living, and both Brendan and I have a great wee life.

I really missed my husband mostly on a Sunday, as he always took us away for a drive after dinner. We would've gone to the seaside or to Lifford Town to their granny's house. We did that for years, so you can imagine I didn't know what to do with my Sundays. However, I managed, and I used to take the pram up to the cemetery with about seven of them hanging on to it. We would have visited the daddy's grave and go around the whole cemetery looking at all the old graves. It's a couple of miles walk, so we were tired by the time we were finished. I didn't mind the late evenings when it got dark. The children would've settled down to do their homework. I was fortunate enough that I could help them with it, but it wasn't long until the older children were able to take care of the younger ones. The years then seemed very long and distant, with nothing to look forward to, with no holidays and still no money. It took the housekeeping money to feed us all, and not one complained. I felt sorry that I couldn't give any of them pocket money. After the youngest was about five years old, I started to work at night. I got £6 per week, and this helped a lot. Kay used to put the wee ones to bed and I didn't get home until 11.00pm. The smaller shops stayed open late in those days.

I was getting a bit better off now; two of my family started working and each in their turn got good jobs. However, by the same token, each of them left home and got married. Those were the unhappiest days of my life. The day that each member of my family got married, I broke my heart about them in turn, but I have no grudges against their partners, they are all first class. The feeling of loss at the time was hard to bear, but I got used to their being out of the house. I accepted my loss as a 'gain', all my daughters-in-law are lovely girls and each of them made me feel welcome in their homes. As for my sons-in-law, they, too, are great. They are very close to me.

I was very fortunate in getting acquainted with some wonderful people. The thought of leaving them behind hurts me a lot, as dying I can't accept, and to leave my children is hard to bear. If there were a way that I could see them from time to time, I would be a happy woman. I will try hard to watch over them. It is a bond between a mother and her children and it is something that grows stronger as time goes on. It doesn't ease off, and no matter whether they are married or not, it is still there. I have always been a very deep thinker and have some lovely dreams; they always seem to be about my children when they were young. All of my thoughts are based on my family.

My family have done me proud and I know that their father would be the proudest father of all if he were alive today. I am determined to carry on with my daily chores and work in the piano shop. I will keep going until the good Lord says, 'Kathleen, that's enough.' And I hope when he calls me that he will give me one more trip down to Paddy's Wood. But alas, I won't hear the voices calling: 'There's a Fire in the Wood.'

Shared Memories

I am most grateful to the Derry people who allowed me to adapt and share the following short reflections of their own childhood memories which may help you recall some past, happier days of your own. These stories were originally included in a publication entitled *From Acorn to Oak* compiled by Stephen Kelly and produced by Guildhall Press on behalf of the NSPCC in 1998.

Growing Up in Foyle Road
Sister Anna, Community Leader

I remember the house where I was born; it was 120 Foyle Road, that lovely road which wound its way alongside the silvery waters of the Foyle River, famed in song and story. Sandwiched between the road and the river, the Great Northern Railway (GNR) snaked southwards, its steam trains chugging away to Belfast and Dublin.

Many of the people who lived on Foyle Road were employed in the GNR and some of the railway men lodged with the good people who lived there; kindly, friendly, generous people, whose hearts, like their hall doors, were always open and welcoming. This was a tight-knit community, ready to lend a helping hand to the old, the sick and the needy. I was happy to belong to such a fine neighbourhood.

Sadness often visited our street. This was in the days when children suffered from diphtheria, scarlatina and polio. TB was commonplace. Accidents at work also took their toll. I vividly remember when one of our neighbours, Willie Connor, a linesman on the railway, had a very serious accident, losing his leg and subsequently his life. The whole street was stunned by his untimely death. My own family was devastated, as he and his wife had taken my newly wed parents under their wing when they first came to Foyle Road. The kindly older couple had lost their youngest daughter a short time before. It seemed such a cruel blow of fate. That was my first brush with life's tragedy and I remember the grief to this day.

In those days, there were two big shirt factories on Foyle Road: the Star, and Tillie and Henderson's. Workers came there from all parts of the city. As a child, I enjoyed watching the crowds of women of all ages, surging up and down the street to and from work, their chattering and singing and laughter filling the air with vitality. These women were the backbone of Derry. Many of them had to run their homes, manage the money and look after their families while holding down a job, as many women still do.

In later years, working in Shantallow, I was to meet some of them again, now retired and enjoying their hard-earned leisure. It was good to sit and talk to them, reflecting on times past and recalling events they had long forgotten. These were skilled needlewomen, second to none. In those days, there were over six thousand people employed in shirt making, and Derry shirts were famous the world over. The women took great pride in the perfection and finish of their work. It is sad to see that professionalism and skill lost forever to profit making.

The war years were very hard on our parents: rationing of food, fuel and clothes was a big problem. As children, we just accepted our lives and got on with it. When the air-raid sirens wailed their warnings, fear gripped our parents' hearts. Some fled to the open fields at Brae Head, but we all squeezed into the cubby-hole under the stairs for shelter. Later in the war, we sought safety with other families in the purpose-built air-raid shelters on the street. At length, our parents took us to Ardmore to live, unable to stand the strain.

A family from England came to stay in our house because Foyle Road was safer for them. This was common practice at the time, and lasting bonds of friendship were formed between the evacuees and Irish families.

Foyle Road was in the Long Tower parish – a parish unrivalled in this city – at the heart of which stands St Columba's Church. Its magnificent marble sanctuary, stained-glass windows and ancient walls have witnessed the celebration of the sacraments for centuries. The seasons of the year were marked by many festivals, but in Long Tower the feast of Saint Columba (our patron saint) on 9 June took pride of place. Every parishioner wore an oak leaf and when the bands in the procession trumpeted the hymn *St Columba, St Columba, Holy patron of our town, While thy children sing thy praises, From thy throne in heaven look down*, our hearts swelled with pride.

The people of the Long Tower were the very salt of the earth. It was 'care in the community' perfected, for although there was poor housing, overcrowding, unemployment and low wages, their generous-hearted and unstinting support of one another saw them through hard times together. It was there I found the inspiration, energy and enthusiasm for the work in which I had the privilege to be involved in later years.

School days were happy days for me, full of seasonal games, from skipping and hopscotch in the spring, to sleighing and sliding in the winter. I went first to the Long Tower Girls, then to the Preparatory School in Artillery Street and finally to Thornhill.

The bigger girls took care of the little ones at school, and while they were allowed to share in the games, their elders kept them in their place. I can remember taking a wee girl by the hand to school. Her name was Alice, and I looked on her as a little sister.

Ours was a mixed community on Foyle Road. We had no need for a Community Relations Council. Our joys, our sorrows, our pain, our pleasures were shared. Children played together. Adults of all religions and none socialised together. We went to watch the Twelfth of August celebrations, enjoying the glamour of the bands and the banners, while they came to the annual Long Tower Carnival. In our street I learnt tolerance and how to live in harmony with your neighbours, lessons that have stood me in good stead throughout my life.

I could write a book about my city, its music, its singers, its choirs, its concerts and pantomimes. I love its old Walls, the beautiful Guildhall, our two fine cathedrals, the old convent in Pump Street, the lovely parks, the city centre so cruelly laid waste in the 1970s, but thanks be to God, living and thriving once again.

These are my memories of Derry, the town I love well, and its people that I love even more. I'm glad to be able to share them with you.

Eccentrics Or What?
Gerry Anderson, Broadcaster

Most people, when asked, say that they dream in black and white… a dream in colour is, apparently, comparatively rare. I'm sure there must be some perfectly adequate psychological reason for this, but I wonder would it explain why I remember my childhood only in black and white.

I had a very happy childhood growing up in Derry in the 1950s, but for reasons I can't fathom, I don't remember any bright colours. Everything was grey, charcoal grey or black. Cars were black or grey, clothes were white, grey or black, buildings were grey and the people seemed happy and friendly, but still grey.

As I trawl my memory for a trace of colour, the only thing that comes to me are the bright colours of Gretta Torrens's parrot that used to sit in its cage outside her pet shop in Little James Street and curse at the Scottish people who passed her door en route from the boat to the Lough Swilly bus station in Great James Street. I think it was eventually brought permanently indoors at the behest of the RUC, who received a number of complaints… the parrot spoke excellent Chaucerian English.

We used to buy new suits out of Burton's to wear for the closing of the annual retreat in St Eugene's Cathedral. We had a choice of three colours – black, charcoal grey and grey. I was an early dandy and always went for the exotic charcoal grey. I suppose it's not unusual really – nobody wore bright colours then. Maybe it was considered unmanly, or slightly risqué. Bright-coloured clothes couldn't be got anyway. At that time, if a man wanted to buy a red shirt, he would probably have to fly to Naples.

I used to think about this quite a lot, and just when I thought it was all just in my imagination, I saw an old photograph taken at the Brandywell of a crowd watching a football match in the '30s. There were thousands of people at the match, all wearing caps, and they seemed to be wearing identical clothes. Of course, the photograph was in black and white, but you could tell that everybody was wearing dull clothes.

There was one startling exception. Standing in the front row of a section of the crowd was a figure that stood out

Gerry Anderson in the 1980s, getting wet for charity, proving he too can be eccentric!

Hawker Lynch, seated bottom left, at a match in the Brandywell, 1935.
(Courtesy David Bigger collection)

immediately. Amid the homogeneous mass was a man dressed from head to toe in bright clothes – jumper, sports coat, cap, shoes, trousers and socks – all bright, but not, seemingly, all white, leading one to suspect that perhaps his jumper and socks, and maybe his trousers, were yellow or, who knows, may even be green or red!

I searched frantically for a name in the explanatory caption underneath and it read: *Photograph taken at the Brandywell in 1938, featuring a large section of the crowd watching Derry City play Glenavon in a very well-supported Irish League match. Prominent in the picture is the flamboyant figure of local eccentric, Hawker Lynch.*

So, there it was. You could tell he was an eccentric because he was wearing bright clothes. Maybe I was right after all – if you wore anything bright, you were considered mad! Hawker Lynch wouldn't merit a second glance in the Brandywell these days – he was ahead of his time.

I didn't know Hawker Lynch, but I knew his sidekick, Johnny Cuttems, who survived up until comparatively recently. I was born and raised in Sackville Street, and Johnny, for one reason or another, used to spend a lot of his time sitting alone on a doorstep at one of the entrances to Hogg and Mitchell's factory at the top of our street. He would sit there most nights, not doing anything in particular and, being about eight years old at the time, I was a little afraid of him, as I used to have to pass him on my way back and forward to my Uncle James's sweet shop round the corner.

One winter's night about nine o'clock, I edged nervously past him and he called me over. 'C'mere, young fella,' he said. (I've shortened this for obvious reasons. Those of you who remember Johnny Cuttems's severe speech impediment will realise that the act of saying *C'mere, young fella* took a considerable amount of time and effort.) 'Look at that moon,' he said, gazing skywards. I did what I was told with some trepidation. 'It's a full moon,' he said. 'You can make out every feature with your naked eye. Do you believe in the man in the moon?'

'I never thought about it much,' I stuttered truthfully.

'Well, you should,' he said. 'If there was a man in the moon, he'd have to have food to live on, wouldn't he?'

'Yes, I suppose he would,' I answered.

'Well, use your imagination. Look at the moon and tell me if there's anything there that looks like food.'

I looked at the moon. It was huge.

'Look over to the left hand side, near the top. Does that not look like an apple tree to you?'

I looked hard. He was right. There was a kind of outline thing that did vaguely resemble a tree or plant. I told him so.

'There you are,' he laughed. 'Now look down at the bottom right hand side. Couldn't that be a rabbit?'

You know, I could see something that looked a bit like something on four legs.

'That's the man in the moon off to a good start. Plenty of apples and a bit of rabbit for his dinner,' Johnny said, warming to the exercise. He went on to point out other imaginary objects that he saw on the surface of the lunar landscape that could be of use to the man in the moon, and I found myself sitting down beside him on the doorstep, looking for something on the surface that had escaped his attention. We sat there talking for an hour until I heard the voice of my mother calling me. I had been sent out for a pint of milk and this was no way to go about it. I tore myself away, bought the milk, and said goodnight to him on my way back home. He nodded, waved airily and stared at the moon again.

I didn't think about it much at the time, but now I realise that Johnny Cuttems had made me study the surface of the moon as I had never studied it before. Of course, he was only an eccentric... just like his mate, Hawker Lynch.

Snapshots
John Keanie, Former Town Clerk &
Chief Executive, Derry City Council

Recalling childhood memories has reached epidemic proportions in Ireland. Is our present so complex, our future so unpredictable, that we need to resort to the comfort of the past? The past is static and unthreatening. It can be observed, sifted, analysed, even lied about if there are no witnesses. We can manipulate our account of it to squeeze out sympathy, to explain away our faults and to excuse our actions. It had never occurred to me to write about my childhood.

Nevertheless, thinking back, recalling incidents and thoughts from long ago can be mildly habit forming, even for the self-professed sceptic. So what I'm going to give you is presented simply as a random selection of snapshot memories, some funny – at least to me – some sad, some slightly wistful but, hopefully, not mawkish. They are not meant to build to any great conclusion and are neither organised by theme nor arranged chronologically. Why these particular memories popped out is perhaps the only mystery of this piece. One thing which is common to them all is their clarity to me, their near presence as if they had happened yesterday. It makes me doubt if time can truly be a healer, or even a distancer, and makes me selfishly glad that the horrors of abuse or neglect never visited me to brutalise me, to desensitise me or to be perpetuated like some curse handed down from generation to generation.

Second day at school. Four years old. It is January, snowing, as we walk up Glendermott Road and my skinny little legs are freezing in my short trousers. I don't want to go to school and I'm pretty forceful about it. My mother, in panic at this sudden insurgence, slaps my legs. So many years later and she has never forgotten it, nor forgiven herself; beautiful piece of blackmail!

I'm five years old, at the corner of Bond's Place and Bond Street. It's 8.00pm and I'm sitting on the pavement with some friends. We've been trying out cursing, maybe for the first time, and along comes da to bring me in for bed. 'You're a big shite!' I say; I suppose bravado carried me away. That was just before I got carried away to bed – I'm lucky my parents weren't as strict as some of the other boys' mas and das.

I've been sitting quietly on the old horsehair sofa at the front window in 6 Bond's Place. No-one else is in the room and it's starting to get dark. The sideboard is on the wall opposite me and there's a hole in the corner of the skirting board underneath it. This is where the little mice scurry out nervously for crumbs and whatever else is going. I like them. At least I prefer them to the silverfish in the damp cupboard under the stairs, or the cockroaches that creep and stop, creep and stop, across the green linoleum. I wish the grown-ups wouldn't set those nasty traps. The noise, when they snap, scares me, and the dark blood makes me sad.

Cousin Drew, Auntie Patsy and Uncle Walter are brilliant. I'm ten and Drew is seven and a half. We are standing in Patrick Street, about to get on the Swilly bus for Fahan. We've got a picnic basket and I've borrowed a pair of grey woollen swimming trunks. I hope they fit. The pavement is hot and I hope they've got plenty of drinks.

I'm thirteen now and Walter has just had a win on the horses. He's taking me with them for a week in Portrush; told you they were brilliant!

I'm sitting in All Saints' Sunday school. I'm twelve and I've been thinking about this religion business. It's not for me. Twice on Sunday means two round trips from Mourne Drive to Clooney Terrace, no matter what the weather's like, and anyway, how can a king start a Church because he wants a divorce? When I'm fourteen and in long trousers I can make my announcement.

The rest of the class is laughing at me. I'm in the headmaster's class at Rossdowney Primary School and I've just been told off for betraying my ignorance. I thought a submarine cable was for tying up a submarine. I wish it were dinnertime. They'll forget about it in the afternoon.

We've just got a Pye radio. It's red and cream Bakelite, and has a round dial with a pointer on it which points to words like Hilversum and Luxembourg. I could sit up all night with this, listening to the songs about school hops and dancing and girls. I'm going to get a guitar and play in a rock-'n'-roll band.

I left my granda to the Irish Street bus stop and I'm walking home, looking at the half-crown he gave me. He seemed very sad and he told me to do well in my Junior exams tomorrow. Maybe his artificial leg was hurting him. That was Churchill's fault. He only ever swears if he mentions Churchill. He says he's an old bastard. He's not my full granda. That was James Wallace, who died in the First World War. That war took my other granda, Francis Keanie, too. Not many boys have had three grandas! My da says a lot of people who got a battlefield commission were shot. They only had a pistol and they had to be out of the trenches first to lead the men.

Granda's dead. Auntie Lena found him. He was sprawled across the bed. She says he must have felt ill and was trying to get into bed. Lena is hurting because he died on his own while she was at the factory. He had the artificial leg half off. I wonder did he think about Churchill.

It's October 1962 and I'm cycling home from games at Springtown. I've sneaked out early because I want to be at home if they drop the bomb. I wonder will I make it. I think three o'clock is the deadline. Kennedy is tough, but Khrushchev seemed mad enough to keep going. I wonder what it will feel like. I hope I get home.

I'm fourteen now and I've got the long trousers. The suit is new and I'm soaked walking up from All Saints. Ma, I've got something to tell you…

The White Horse Inn
Colum Arbuckle, Producer, Radio Foyle

The White Horse Inn at Campsie has been a familiar landmark to travellers of the main Derry to Limavady road for centuries, but on 1 June 1948 it was quite a different place to the prestigious hotel we know today. That was the date my father, mother and myself took up residence in the old Inn that had been on the site for centuries. It was just before my first birthday, and for my parents, who had been living in rented rooms since they got married, it seemed like a dream come true. My father was a barman by trade, and after he served his time in John O'Donnell's Ulster House, he was looking around for a better position.

'The job was advertised in the *Derry Journal*,' he recalled, 'and it said that there was a free house with it, so I applied and after being interviewed by Johnny Whiteside, who was the owner at the time, and Father Kielt who, I suppose, was looking for a barman of the proper character, I got the position of resident barman of The White Horse Inn at £4 a week.'

The original Inn had, for hundreds of years, been a stopping place for horse-drawn coaches on their way to and from Derry and Coleraine, and in its day was probably quite a luxurious dwelling. Passengers could get a rest, a bite to eat and a drink in the bar while waiting for the horses to be changed. This building was our free house, which came with the job, but, as it turned out, it wasn't quite what we had expected on first reading the advertisement.

There was another family called Cooke living in it. They lived upstairs and we had two rooms and a shared kitchen and hall downstairs. The structure of the building hadn't changed much since the coaching days, but it was nearing the end of its days – and looked it. There was no running water, no electricity, and the only heat was from a big open fire in the living-room. Light was provided by an old Tilley lamp that had to be refilled with paraffin oil and primed two or three times before bedtime on winter evenings.

The bar was lit by gas lights from bottled gas, and glasses had to be washed under a cold tap in the backyard. The toilet for both the house and bar was a primitive, outside, dry affair, consisting of little more than a wall for the gentlemen and a bucket for the ladies.

The bar opened from ten o'clock in the morning to nine in the evening but closed for an hour at 6.00pm while my father got his tea and, because he was working a six-day week and was entitled to one half-day, it closed on a Tuesday at 2.00pm. Any locals who wanted sustenance on a Tuesday evening had to go further afield. Stout, from bottles only, was one shilling and sixpence – cheaper than the return bus fare to Derry.

It sounds like a pretty primitive place to live in and I suppose, by today's standards, it was. But expectations were not as high then, and when you compare it to living in one room in a two-up, two-down terraced house in the middle of the city, the space, privacy and freedom of a country house with your livelihood right next door must have, to my parents, seemed a pretty attractive lifestyle indeed.

'Do you know this? Six years we lived there, and it was really the happiest years of my life,' my mother always told us. 'There was something exciting going on in it every day. The people in the neighbourhood were the friendliest I had ever met. We came into it as strangers and we were just made at home. Every house we went to we were treated like royalty. Everybody made that much of you. I tried to make the house as comfortable as possible, and while Joe was working the bar, I decorated the rooms as best I could. I scraped away the old lime from the walls and then papered them, and got some plywood from a man down the road and got the old kitchen panelled.'

'The door was never locked,' dad recollected, 'and the house never emptied. As often as not, when I closed the bar at teatime, any customers who were still there would come in and join us for a bite to eat. Most of the locals, who were coming or going on the Derry bus or just passing by on their way to the shops in Eglinton, would drop into the house for a cup of tea; and even at night, after the bar closed, few would go home before calling in for a chat. One thing I was very strict about was the bar licensing laws, and there was never any drink sold outside opening hours, nor was there ever any drink allowed in the house. I remember one time two policemen came to the door about ten o'clock at night and said they had information that illegal drinking was going on in the house. I brought them in and there were about half a dozen men sitting around the big table, eating soup. The policemen looked around and satisfied themselves that nothing was going on and were about to leave when the sergeant asked me what the lovely smell was.

'That's Kathleen's soup, I told him. Would you like some?

'"I would," said the sergeant, and joined us for a bowl before heading back on duty.'

I don't remember too much about the first couple of years in the Inn, but I certainly have many memories of later times. It was a magical place for a young boy with a vivid imagination. In the old stables, still there from the coaching days, bandits and ghouls lurked on dark days, and on brighter ones, camp could be made with fellow cowboys or Roman forts could be defended against barbarian invaders. The garden was huge and contained all sorts of fruits like gooseberries, raspberries, apples, pears and plums. Climbing and swinging apparatus were constructed on the many trees, using old bits of harness and pieces of broken stout crates. The Black Braes wasn't far away – as exciting to me then as any continental seaside is to today's youngsters.

We always had a dog and, for a while, I had a pet piglet. It would follow me around everywhere and come when called, just like a pup. It even pulled a 'chariot' down the garden on a couple of occasions. Someone had given it to my mother to fatten and get ready to sell for slaughter, but by the time it had reached the desired weight, it was so tame that no-one had the heart to send it to its predestined fate. It stayed with us until we got a farmer to take it. Of course, he had to promise not to kill it before it was allowed to leave The White Horse Inn.

It all sounds like an idyllic country life, meandering through the hours, days and weeks at the pace of a lazy meadow stream. Not a bit of it, according to my mother. At Campsie, even getting in the weekly groceries was a complicated affair. 'I had to phone the XL Stores in Derry from the pay phone in the bar and they would deliver them the next time the van was in the area. The All Cash Store mobile shop would also come around on a Tuesday and a Friday, and occasionally Quigg's lorry would come around with fruit and vegetables. We got our milk, eggs and potatoes from Lowry's farm across the road. Sam Lowry was a preacher and would just as soon deliver a sermon as a ticking off to his workers. The potato-pickers liked the sermons better, as it gave them a brief rest from their back-breaking work.'

There was never a dull moment in the bar. The customers were a strange mixture of locals and British Army, Navy and Air Force personnel from the nearby married quarters. In the evening, most would arrive on bicycles, which they leaned three and four deep outside the bar and the house. At closing time, sorting out who owned which bicycle often led to minor altercations.

There was no form of heating in the public house except a coal fire, but Johnny Whiteside wouldn't buy coal for it. 'Joe has plenty there on the top shelf to keep you warm,' he would say if anyone complained.

My dad was involved in an elaborate deception, one evening, that not only fooled the drinkers, but also half of Campsie and a good portion of the residents of Eglinton village.

'There was a character who used to frequent the bar who fancied himself as a bit of a ladies man, but he had been a bit down on his romantic luck for a few years and was constantly being teased by the locals. He decided that it was time to re-establish his reputation, so he enlisted my help in an elaborate plot, which had to be carried out with split-second timing to make it work. He passed the word around that he had a date with a beautiful woman, but he refused to reveal anything about her except that he was to meet her outside the White Horse at eight o'clock one summer evening. He positioned himself outside the bar at about quarter to eight and, of course, anyone who was inside came out to see who this mystery woman was. I was well out of sight down the Donnybrewer Road dressed as a woman. I was small and of slight build, so I was able to get away with it. On the stroke of eight, I mounted a borrowed ladies bike and cycled around the comer into full view of the waiting onlookers. As soon as our man saw me, he jumped on his bike, and the two of us cycled off as fast as we could towards Eglinton. When we got there, we did a couple of circuits of the village before we disappeared. He went back home by a different route and I managed to slip back to the bar and get changed. It was years after before anyone realised they had all been fooled.'

There was another occasion when one of the bar patrons dressed up as a woman and tried to scare the men going outside to the toilet by pretending to be a ghostly apparition. Many would say, though, that there were already enough unearthly spirits around the White Horse Inn without someone having to act the part. Most locals would swear the building was haunted.

One night, just about a year before we moved in, there were a number of men playing cards around the big table in the front room. A round was dealt, but every card inexplicably fell face up. The players – and this story was told to mum and dad directly by them, for they still drank in the bar – tried again, but the same thing happened. They dealt a third hand, but when the cards again all landed face up, the men lifted the deck and, without saying a word to each other, left the Inn. Cards were never again played around that table nor in that room.

While we were living in the house, we were being constantly asked about ghosts, and there were even occasions when people gathered outside to try and catch a glimpse of a horse-drawn carriage which was said to appear at certain times of the year. We neither saw nor heard anything at all until one cold winter's night, when we were sure that the devil himself had come to sup at The White Horse Inn.

When my mother told the tale, it always brought a chill over the cosiest of company. 'Well, that night, I'll never forget it. We were terrorised and so were George and Mary Cooke up the stairs. I heard what I thought was like a step… first in the hall. I wakened Joe. Then it went up the stairs… thump… thump… thump… very slow. When it got to the top, it came down again… step… step… step. Joe wouldn't get up and neither would George up the stairs. Not one of us would get up to look. We were all riveted to our beds. The next morning, the mystery of the night visitor was revealed when a large potato, half-eaten by a rat, was found lying in the hall at the bottom of the stairs. The rodent had obviously been trying to get the spud to some secluded part of the house and had managed to lift it up the stairs, step by step – thump, thump, thump – and just when it got it to the top of the staircase, it lost control and it bounced back down again – step, step, step.'

That particular rat wasn't the only one to give us grief in the old house. They infested the place and we all had many a close encounter. Mum trapped one behind a cupboard, one time, and managed to spear it with a poker. She thought it was dead, but as soon as she withdrew the weapon, it jumped down and scuttled towards the back door, only to meet a swift end in the jaws of the family dog. The rats had a particular liking for a cavity behind the big open fireplace. At night, you could see them running between holes in the back of the grate, and in the garden, at night, they could be heard scurrying to their hiding places as soon as the back door opened.

Someone once told my dad that if you burned a rat alive, its squeals during its death throes would drive the others away. He caught one in a cage and roasted it on a bonfire just outside the back door. The ritual didn't work and he told me years later, 'It was the cruellest thing I ever did.'

Like the unfortunate creature, we all nearly met untimely ends during our stay at the White Horse. I came close on two occasions. The first time was when a large delivery lorry missed me by inches as it sped along the main road. The second time was inside the house but was no less dramatic. I was in bed in the back bedroom, ill at the time, and the ceiling, an old, heavy plaster and lath affair, fell in around me. The first part blocked the door from the inside and my mother couldn't get to me. She ran to the bar to get help and some men managed to get the back window open and pass me out through it, seconds before the whole lot came down on top of the bed. Mum always said that if I hadn't been rescued when I was, I would never have spoken again.

My mum's near encounter with the grim reaper happened one Christmas Eve when she was seven months pregnant with my sister Siobhan. My father was in bed, very ill, and that morning, she had just about managed to get the heavy front shutters off, open the bar and hold the fort until a replacement barman arrived. Later, she was down in the front room, standing on the big table to hang some washing up on an inside line. This was the same table that had been the scene of the card players' eerie experience some years earlier. When she was getting down, she fell and landed on her back on the old flagstone floor. She couldn't get to her feet, and dad was so ill that he was unable to rise out of bed to assist. The Cooke family, who lived upstairs, had a radio on and didn't hear her cries for help. She had to crawl on her hands and knees back to the kitchen and somehow manage to pull herself up on a chair. She was so badly hurt, however, that she couldn't even go to the fire and remove a pot of tapioca that she had boiling there. She had no option but to sit and watch it boil and burn the pot.

Later that day, she had recovered sufficiently to go to the bar and call the doctor. Fortunately, she had suffered no damage to her pregnancy and nothing was broken, but dad, on the other hand was, by this time, very seriously ill, and the doctor suspected meningitis. He wanted to shift him into the hospital, but because it was Christmas Eve, he decided to wait. 'That was the loneliest Christmas I ever had,' mum remembered. 'We had planned to spend the holidays with my mother in Donegal and Santa had been instructed to deliver his presents there. I hadn't one bite to eat in the house and practically no money to get anything, even if I had been able to go shopping. I did try and get a chicken, but there were just none available. I didn't know what I was going to do, but luckily, a regular in the bar heard of my plight and offered me a duck, which I was glad to accept. Colum took sick that evening also, and I sat by myself on Christmas Day, eating the duck with the tears blinding me.' Dad was shifted into hospital on Boxing Day and, thankfully, recovered. Siobhan was delivered with no complications the following February. She wasn't born in the White Horse, but she was the last newborn baby to be brought into it.

In 1954, my father was offered a better-paying job in Ebrington House in the Waterside and we had to give up the country residence. We left on 1 June 1954, exactly six years to the day from the date we moved in. We went from the spacious 'luxury' of The White Horse Inn to one room at 7 Limavady Road, the winter residence of Cullen's Amusements. For me, a boisterous seven-year-old, it was like leaving one Disney World and finding another one just around the corner. But that's another story.

Years Ago
Claude Wilton, Retired Solicitor

My childhood was comfortable. I was born in 1917 in the old houses in Eden Terrace and was the younger of two children; my sister was four years older. I went to Foyle College, then in Lawrence Hill, and, on the first day, sat on my schoolbag, containing a couple of bananas (my lunch). Some weeks later, my blazer was wet and all dirty after a fall, and I hung it over a stove and burnt it. It was not an auspicious start to my school career.

The area where I spent my school years was well mixed in every sense of the word and, unlike today, I cannot recall any time of sectarianism, though there was some poverty, and many houses were overcrowded.

We had happy days, playing football on a vacant piece of grassless ground near Richmond Hill (now full of garages) and my late father, who was in the timber business, supplied the goal posts. Occasionally, we played away fixtures at Pat's Field on Foyle Road. Rugby was the only game permitted in Foyle, and although I preferred soccer, I enjoyed the train journeys to play matches at various schools in the province. I could never understand why children were sent in almost all cases to segregated schools. Unfortunately, this is still largely the case.

A lasting memory of those hard times in the '20s and '30s was watching people handing over a docket for a free meal at a charity function at Christmas; my mother was Mayoress for some years and we helped at this function. I think this was the first time I realised that the community was unfairly divided. It led to my later involvement in the Civil Rights Movement, to try and ensure that each child received a fair opportunity in life.

In the long summer nights, it was pleasant to cycle to Fahan for a dip, or a bit of cricket or football in the old City of Derry Cricket Grounds at Duncreggan. Later, we would watch and play in the Summer League.

Although many aspects of my schooldays have faded in my memory, I am glad to say that I never encountered any bitterness. I hope and trust I have grown up to be broadminded and tolerant, if nothing else.

Happy Times
Larry Hasson, Austins of The Diamond

My da was a big man, a sheep farmer from the mountain of Mullahash in Feeny, and my mother was a small woman from the same town. They fell in love and eloped to Scotland, where they got married. They came back to Derry, where I was born in 1910. I had three sisters and a brother. I had a very happy childhood and went to school in Bridge Street and then to the Christian Brothers. I played football with the great Jimmy Kelly, a former international, and also in the street.

I enjoyed the summer holidays when we went out to my Aunt Mary's in Feeny for six weeks. It was great helping them with the turnips, cutting the corn and digging big spuds. We would go to the mountain to cut turf, and my Aunt Mary brought us tea and scones for lunch.

We went to Feeny by Robert's bus. If the bus was full, we were put on the top, our feet dangling over – what a view! It was great when you were going around corners. The weather seemed to be always dry. Those were the days

Larry Hasson of Austins, a spritely ninety-four years young.

my Uncle Roddy always took me in the horse and cart to all the fairs, where he bought and sold sheep and cattle, and then into the pub for a drink over a sale; I got lemonade. The holidays finished all too quickly; then back home again.

Every Friday night was pay night; my da always gave my brother and me sixpence, and I spent fourpence at the pictures. A penny for a bar of chocolate, and a penny for two-and-a-half Wild Woodbine fags. When cutting the fag in half, the shopkeeper would squeeze it so much that you could hardly smoke it. Half a fag for Pathé News, one for the comedy, and one for parts four and five of the big picture.

My da's hobby was shooting, so he often brought me out to Mullahash to shoot moorfowl. He carried me on his back, in his bare feet, and we would tramp for hours, and then stop for something to eat. When I was about fifteen, he got me a gun from my uncle and taught me how to shoot. I remember shooting a hare and a moorhen, and I nearly shot myself on one occasion. I had walked into a green, marshy bog – gun at the ready – after a moorhen, and sunk almost two feet and the gun went off. Those were very happy times.

An army helicopter helps to replace the cross on top of St Columb's Cathedral spire after repairs were completed to the roof in the 1970s. Background includes Bishop Street, Fountain Estate and St Columb's College. (Courtesy David Bigger collection)

Derry Wans up the Town

A wee sample of the many local inhabitants who have enriched Derry down the decades.

Top left: Plenty of time to sit and stare in sunny Waterloo Square in 2004 – L to R: Gerald Breslin, Eddie Matheson, Swalla O'Neil and John Daly. Top right: Aidan Heaney, the local stage and play actor at the bottom of Waterloo Street, contentedly puffing away on his Peterson briar pipe. Below: Michael Gallagher, Don 'Beaver' Riley, Richard Smith, Danny 'Spassy' McGilloway and Lorne Riley.

Eamon Melaugh, well-known voluntary community worker and India Aid Relief organiser, finds time to stroll with his friends Jamesie McMullen and Paddy McColgan in the Strand Road in 2003.

Four retired Derrymen with vastly different working backgrounds sitting in Waterloo Place in 2003 listening to the latest bars from Frank Boyle. Left to right: musician Bertie Barratt; former Glasgow Celtic footballer Tom Hippsley; steel erector Barney Gillespie; and egg packer and distributor Joe Barr.

Above: Mamie Redden with her daughter Helen, Mary Lyttle and Pauline Doherty. Left: Mickey McGuinness, respected historian, writer, singer, footballer and storyteller. Below: Tommy Maguire, former Midlands Railway employee, behind the counter of his second-hand historical artefacts shop in Carlisle Road.

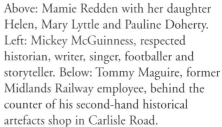

Left: Seamus Ball, Derry's favourite stage, film and television actor, being trained by his collie dog at the Quayside pedestrian walkway in 2004. Above middle: Raymond Quigg, the Rocking Chair king, taking in the fresh air in the Diamond in 2003. Above right: Charlie Morrison out for his daily constitutional in 2003.

Waiting for their lunches in Pilot's Row Community Centre are: Paddy Harkin, Mickey Roddy, Tony O'Donnell and Brendan McMenamin.

Top left: Marty McMenamin, former Nelson Street dweller, going into the Long Tower Church to say a wee prayer in June 2004. Top right: Patsy Durnin, local historian, author and musician, getting his head shired beside the Foyle. Above left: Whitey O'Neil posing on Shipquay Street. Above right: Jackie 'Aikie' Coyle who graced Derry's dancehalls for many years.

Afterword

A few years ago I began writing down my memories of growing up in Derry, mostly for my children and family. I never imagined that one day I would be finishing a trilogy recording many of the experiences, escapades and people I encountered in the city from 1937 until the early 1970s. These memories and stories reflected the lives and conditions of so many Derry people during the same era until things changed dramatically for us all at the beginning of the 1970s.

I consciously avoided writing about the so-called troubles through which so many unfortunate families endured painful experiences and are still suffering to the present day. I felt that I didn't have the right or ability or permission to write about the traumas and horrific ordeals in other people's lives. My own young family of six boys and a girl somehow miraculously escaped any physical harm even though we never escaped the frightening and degrading early morning raids and house searches by the army and RUC.

I have savoured the many hours of remembering and writing down my thoughts as well as other Derry people's little personal tales in my books and hope the readers enjoyed having their own memories stirred as they browsed through the old photographs and meandering yarns of the inhabitants of the long-gone streets of our beautiful city of Derry. It was a nice opportunity for me also to renew contact with many of my old acquaintances and to make new friendships with many warm-hearted well-wishers who approached me since I began writing my short pieces on the west bank's social history.

Now that some of my memories are recorded in print, I feel content that I have preserved pictures and written about a few of our more colourful characters and neighbours who made Derry a happier and safer place to grow up in former years. As I sit here now in my easy chair, I can close my eyes and see those people silently moving through the streets or standing at their front doors and hear the many different sounds of street noises and the voices of children at play. I can also smell the smoke coming from the chimney pots as it gets caught in the breeze and is wafted downwards through the streets and my open window... there I go again...